BABY BOOMER SPIRITUALITY

TEN ESSENTIAL VALUES
OF A GENERATION

Craig Kennet Miller

DISCIPLESHIP RESOURCES

MATERIALS FOR GROWTH IN CHRISTIAN FAITH AND LIFE

P.O. Box 189 • Nashville, TN 37202 • Phone (615) 340-7284

Reprinted 1993.

ISBN 0-88177-106-6

Library of Congress Card Catalog No. 91-72143

DR106

ACKNOWLEDGMENTS

To my father, Arthur Kennet Miller, who said I could do anything I set my mind to do . . .

To Vicki Schneider, Ray Anderson, Craig Gallaway, Peggy Bray, Connie Ashworth, and Neal Montgomery, whose insights and suggestions helped shape this book . . .

To my friends at Santigo Hills for their prayers . . .

To my mother, Joyce Jean Miller, who taught me to always have faith . . .

To my wife, Ivy, whose support never ceases to amaze me . . .

And to my daughter, Jasmine Ying, who gives me hope for the future . . .

. . . I say thank you.

CONTENTS

INTRODUCTION

America is undergoing its own revolution. While its ideals of democracy and freedom are breaking out across the globe, American society is moving into a new era. This American revolution is based on the slow turn of demographic forces that is transferring power and leadership to the baby boom generation. This generation of 77 million Americans—almost one-third of the population of the United States—was born during the postwar economic boom from 1946 to 1964, and will be ages thirty-six to fifty-four in the year 2000. As we move through the 1990s and head into a new millennium, the baby boom generation will set the agenda for the United States and, thus, for a world that looks to North America for its vision of the future.

This is not an idle claim but is the result of the converging forces of demographics, economics, and technology—forces that are bringing North American ideas, values, and beliefs to the forefront of world leadership. In 1989, as revolution broke out in Eastern Europe, it was Thomas Jefferson and Martin Luther King, Jr. who were quoted by the revolutionaries. When Chinese students protested in Tiananmen Square, it was the Goddess of Democracy, modeled after the Statue of Liberty, which stood as the symbol of hope for freedom in China. When Kuwait was overrun by Iraqi forces, it was the United States that had the willpower to return the land to its rightful owners. When Russia broke the shackles of communism, it quickly turned to the United States for aid and guidance as it sought to form its own form of democracy.

In movie theaters and on television screens in virtually every country of the world, U.S. programs and films dominate the market. On radios and tapeplayers in the household of every trendy world teenager, American music—from jazz, to big band, to rap, to pop, to new age—predominates. In the center of every major city in the world, from Moscow to Tokyo, stands a symbol of Americana that baby boomers have idolized from their youth—that great dispenser of American hamburgers, french fries, and milkshakes—the golden arches of McDonald's.

As fashionable as it has been at times to cry out about the decline of America, such decline is not inevitable. The generation that wanted to change the world in the '60s will have real power to do so as a new century dawns in the year 2000. The choices boomers make will affect all areas of American life: business, politics, education, family, and religion. Much of what they decide will depend on how they see themselves and their history. Unlike their parents' generation, who could point to the Depression and to World War II as events that shaped their generation, baby boomers have a cloudier view of their past, punctuated by single events that do not seem to make a whole. Vietnam, Watergate, the Challenger disaster, and the Exxon Valdez oil spill in Alaska do not seem to have any continuity, except as signs of American powerlessness and decline.

There are many ways to look at the baby boom generation—their numbers, their economic clout, their politics—but underneath it all stands their unique worldview, which I call baby boomer spirituality. This spirituality is seen in their music, their lifestyles, their religion, their relationships with one another, and their view of the future.

Spirituality has to do with the nature and the quality of a person's soul, the language and the values of a person's heart, and the attitudes and beliefs of a person's mind, which cause each of us to live out our worldview in the context of a relationship with God, other human beings, and creation. Spirituality transcends all areas of one's being and brings meaning and purpose of life.

In the pages that follow I make no claim to define boomer spirituality in one tight theological or sociological package. Instead, I invite you on a journey of perspective such as baby boomers themselves have taken. This journey will illumine the myths and beliefs, the passions and the pain of generation that has always wanted to make a difference in this world. The first section will focus on the spiritual roots of the boomers, the second on their search for God, and the third on their view of the future.

In many ways this has been a very personal journey for me. I must admit I come to this project with a biased view. As a baby boomer born in 1954, I see world events through the eyes of my generation, and as a Christian pastor I see things through the matrix of modern Christianity, which in many ways has failed to meet the deepest needs of this generation. More than anything else, I come at this book with hope for the future, a future that can be shaped by the values and beliefs that baby boomers hold so dear.

1

SPIRITUAL ROOTS

Over the Rainbow

Somewhere over the rainbow
Blue birds fly.
Birds fly over the rainbow,
Why then, Oh why can't I?

If happy little blue birds fly beyond the rainbow,
Why, Oh why can't I?

Chapter One

BROKENNESS

Two images stand out clearly in my mind when I think of the '60s. The first is the image of my father and me, standing in a long line at the grocery store with three carts filled with canned food and paper goods; it was during the height of the Cuban Missile Crisis. All day my father had hammered plywood over the windows in the basement of our house and had stored water in a trash can in the expectation of a nuclear attack. I remember helping him look at the wood that covered the windows to see if there were any cracks where radiation might seep through if we were hit. It was the first time I had seen him scared. At the grocery store, I realized we were not alone in our fear. All around us were anxious people with shopping carts filled with survival goods. At eight years old it was the first time I felt fearful of the future.

The second image was hearing an explosion and seeing smoke pouring out of the social science wing of my junior high school. It was the day after the assassination of Martin Luther King, Jr. I was on the baseball field during P.E. when all hell broke loose. After the explosion, students began fighting each other, and I ran for the ten-foot fence that surrounded the school. After climbing it, I ran as fast as I could all the way home. It was my first riot, and I was scared to death. I thought I was too young to die.

Like pictures flashing in a psychedelic movie, other images of the '60s and early '70s cloud my memories: John John saluting his father's coffin in the East Room of the White House . . . body bags being lifted off a helicopter in Vietnam . . . Tiny Tim singing "Tiptoe through the Tulips" on *Laugh In* . . . Neil Armstrong stepping onto the moon, saying, "One small step for man, one giant step for mankind."

Martin Luther King, Jr. proclaiming, "I have a dream" . . . King's body on a hotel balcony in Memphis, Tennessee . . . The Beatles singing "I Want to Hold Your Hand" on *The Ed Sullivan Show* . . . Woodstock, hippies, miniskirts, and love beads.

Fires raging during the Watts riots . . . the police chief of Saigon blowing out the brains of a Viet Cong officer with a pistol shot . . .

3

President Johnson holding his dog up by the ears . . . police officers and demonstrators confronting one another outside the Democratic Convention in Chicago . . . Jane Fonda perched behind an anti-aircraft gun in Hanoi.

Tommy Smith and John Carlos raising their fists in a Black Power salute on the victory stand at the Olympics as "The Star-Spangled Banner" was being played . . . Bobby Kennedy giving a victory salute at the Ambassador Hotel in Los Angeles . . . Bobby Kennedy's head being held after he was shot in a dark kitchen passageway.

Charles Manson in handcuffs . . . Hare Krishnas at the airport . . . the bodies of students at Kent State . . . John and Yoko at a bed-in for peace . . . Patty Hearst holding a rifle in front of a Symbionese Liberation banner . . . Richard Nixon boarding a helicopter after resigning from the presidency.

For me, these are not just pictures in a history book—they are part of my childhood. Like playing football with my friends on the street, going to school, and dressing up to go to church on Sundays, these events shaped my understanding of the world and my outlook on life itself.

It was a crazy time to grow up. For me, "normal" was sitting in front of TV with the family at dinner and watching the body counts from Vietnam being reported like scores in a basketball game on the evening news: Americans 10, Viet Cong 230. It was the only game I knew where the winners tried to come up with the lowest score.

Normal was watching race riots in major cities and seeing police officers swinging clubs at black clergymen. It was seeing women burning their bras in protest against a male-dominated society. It was graduating from high school with half your friends going to college and the other half going to Vietnam. It was challenging authority at every turn and believing that everyone over thirty was against us and was trying to wipe us out.

Regardless of politics and religion and ethical dilemmas, it was the baby boomers who went off and died in Vietnam. It was baby boomers who protested and burned draft cards. It was baby boomers who joined the throngs of civil rights activists. And it was baby boomers who were hit by the full impact of these events as they were coming of age.

In a 1987 article in *Business Month*, Aimee I. Stern helps us see the radical changes that baby boomers felt as they were growing up.

Jane is 36 years old, which means she was born in the first wave of the baby boom. In the year she began college, life was arranged into a series of cubicles. Mom stayed home and defined herself through roast beef. Dad went to work and supported his family. Jane wasn't sure she would finish college. No matter. She would meet the man of her dreams, get married, buy a house and have a mortgage and children.

At college, rules were rigid. Men couldn't go upstairs in the dorm even during the day without signing in, and the dorm mother conducted a bed check every night. Three years later men and women lived together in that same dorm. Vietnam took the lives of some of Jane's friends, and her school went wild in protest. In the year that Jane got out of school, the world was a very different place.[1]

My mother says it all started to change when the Beatles appeared on *The Ed Sullivan Show* February 9, 1964. She remembers the shock she felt when she saw the long hair and heard the hard beat of "I Want to Hold Your Hand." She was not alone. Seventy-three million Americans watched *The Ed Sullivan Show.* Sullivan himself had 50,000 ticket requests for a theater that housed only 700 people. In the month preceding the Beatles' appearance, their first single released in America sold 2 million copies, an unprecedented number of sales for the record industry.[2]

The Beatles are considered by some to be the best rock musicians ever. Combining the rhythm of American black music and the unique harmonies of John Lennon and Paul McCartney, they were a music force unequaled in the decade of the '60s. As talented as they were, much of their success had to do with timing. When the Beatles burst on the scene in January and February 1964, America was in the throes of a deep depression, not economic but psychological and spiritual. Two months earlier, on November 22, 1963, the country was rocked by the devastating news that the president, John F. Kennedy, had been shot in Dallas as he was riding in an open convertible limousine in Dealey Plaza.

From Friday afternoon till the funeral service on Monday, the three major networks gave complete, uninterrupted coverage to the events following the assassination. It was the most watched and most covered event of all time, even surpassing the Gulf War. In the midst of that coverage an improbable scene took place. On Sunday morning, as millions of Americans were watching news coverage of Lee Harvey Oswald's transfer to the Dallas County jail, he was fatally shot in the stomach by Jack Ruby in the basement of the Police and Courts Building.

That event, even more than the assassination of Kennedy, began to sow seeds of doubt into the conscience of America. How was it that

Jack Ruby was able to kill Oswald while he was in police custody? Was Ruby acting alone or was he trying to cover up a conspiracy? Why was Oswald silenced forever? What key did he hold to the assassination of one of America's most popular presidents?

On September 24, 1964, ten months after Kennedy's death, the president's Commission on the Assassination of President Kennedy, known as the Warren Commission, presented its final report to President Lyndon B. Johnson. The report contained over 900 pages and included 6,710 footnotes. Along with twenty-six supporting volumes that were released at a later date, the Warren Commission presented the American public with a staggering 20,000 pages of material, containing an amazing 10 million words. Its conclusions were simple:

- Lee Harvey Oswald, acting alone, killed Kennedy.
- Jack Ruby, acting alone, killed Oswald.
- There was no credible evidence of a conspiracy, foreign or domestic.
- Only three shots were fired, all from the Texas School Book Depository Building. One of these bullets passed through Kennedy's neck and then probably through the chest and wrist of Governor Connally. Another shot hit Kennedy's head. Another shot missed.[3]

As convincing as the arguments seemed, Americans were not impressed. After seeing the actual footage of the assassination, and after reading numerous books and seeing various TV news reports on the subject, most people did not trust the conclusions of the Warren Commission. In surveys taken in 1983, it was shown that 80 percent of Americans believed that Kennedy was killed by conspirators. Even more telling was a follow-up question: 70 percent saw no reason to reopen the case to learn the truth.[4]

Kurt Anderson, in an article in *Rolling Stone*, sums up his generation's view of life in this way:

Nowadays, there are two sides to every answer. We don't face facts and, hell, simply decide. No. That would be too instinctual, too easy, too blithe, too unlike us.

Instead we consider every alternative and feel complete enthusiasm for none of them. We postpone. We fret. We second-guess. Whether it's a matter of deciding what to have for lunch (a sandwich? a salad?) or how to spend the rest of our lives (duplicitous corporate scumbag in New York? bad lyric poet in Seattle?), neither a wholehearted yes nor an unequivocal no comes naturally. We say maybe. We try to act on both impulses, to be unsentimental romantics, to work uptown but live downtown or vice versa, to have it all, foreclosing no option. As individuals, and even as a nation, we grow faint at the prospect of absolute commitment, whether it's marriage, or military intervention in the third world, or thirty-year fixed-rate mortgages. . . .

To most of us, every city, every book, practically every way of life is an interesting place to visit, but we wouldn't want to live there. Would we? Ours is a generation comfortably adrift, bobbing on a sea of ambivalence.[5]

What Anderson calls ambivalence, I would call brokenness. It is a feeling that nothing and no one can be trusted, especially oneself. It is a feeling of continually being lost, not believing there is anything to find. It is like trying to walk in the surf at the ocean, with your feet madly trying to find a foothold, but continually slipping off slimy rocks and falling into shifting sand as the waves of change bombard you in a swirl of white foam.

It is living with the conviction that the trust you had in society has been violated. Discovering that the big promise of the American dream offered to you in your childhood turned out to be a broken series of lies, you feel betrayed. Growing up with a belief in all the so-called institutions of society—church, government, education, work, marriage, and family—you realize they have failed you miserably, leaving you totally alone in an uncaring and coldhearted world.

In childhood baby boomers were raised with a set of assumptions about the world in which they lived.

First, they were Americans, citizens of the greatest, most powerful, most generous, and most giving nation on this earth.

Second, anyone could make it in America if one only worked hard enough. Along with this was the firm belief that anyone could become president of the United States.

Third, America's political and economic system was the best in the world, and we must protect ourselves from the Communists.

Fourth, military might would protect us as well as enable us to spread our values throughout the world.

Fifth, the traditional nuclear family of father, mother, and children, with father the breadwinner and mother the housewife, was ordained by God as the norm for all.

Sixth, we had unlimited natural resources and land at our disposal to use as we wished.

Seventh, technology and scientific breakthroughs would provide us with a boundless future and solve all our problems.

Eighth, only America and Russia counted. The rest of the world was divided into spheres of influence, and small countries provided no threat to our superiority.

Ninth, minorities should stay in their place, and the occasional accomplishments of a few of them were a deviation from the norm.

Tenth, by staying in line with what their parents dictated, and through education, the baby boomer generation would have a better life than their parents had, with no depressions, no wars, and all the consumer goods they would ever want.[6]

Furthermore everyone knew that assassinations took place only in banana republics where despots and revolutionaries took power by force. Only in America was the power to rule passed on peacefully from president to president every four years. But from 1960 to 1980, only one president, Jimmy Carter, served a standard four-year term of office. Kennedy lasted 3, Johnson served 5, Nixon 6, and Ford 2.

The oldest baby boomers, who were born in 1946, were seniors in high school when President Kennedy was killed, and were seniors in college when Martin Luther King, Jr. and Robert Kennedy were assassinated. The youngest boomers, born in 1964, were four years old during the assassinations of 1968, ten years old when Nixon resigned in 1974, and fifteen on November 4, 1979 when, as Theodore H. White, in *America in Search of Itself,* says, "a handful of wild people in faraway Iran seized the American Embassy in Teheran, held our emissaries as hostages, and humiliated the proudest nation on earth."[7]

Concerning the aftermath of President Kennedy's assassination, Tom Shachtman and Martha Wolfenstien in *Decade of Shocks,* noted that the assassination affected children and adolescents the most. On the one hand children identified the president as the most important symbol and leader of the government. To them the president was almost a god-like figure. As a result of their perceptions, Kennedy's death was a threat to their security. On the other hand, adolescents were attracted to the youthful and vigorous image of a president who could do no wrong. Killed in his prime in a bloody spectacle before their eyes, their feelings of loss persisted long after the event took place.[8]

But the assassination of the president was just the beginning. The children and the adolescents, the two groups that were identified as feeling the strongest impact from President Kennedy's assassination, made up a part of the baby boomer generation which faced a whole slew of events and issues that shaped their future and their view of themselves. This was especially true of those who Annie Gottlieb calls the "first wave" of the '60s generation, those born between 1944 and

1949. In *Do You Believe in Magic? The Second Coming of the '60s Generation*, she says,

> . . . those born between 1944 and 1949, who came of age in the years 1965-70, are a special generation. Together with smaller numbers born in the late 1930s and early 1940s, this "first wave" was at the epicenter of the cultural earthquake. [They] met the Sixties tide at its flood in their late teens and early twenties. They took the Sixties more seriously and were the most traumatized and transformed.[9]

The "second wave" of the '60s generation, those born from 1950 to 1957, were still young enough to adapt to the changes their older brothers and sisters saw as a threat or a revelation. Though confused and impressed by the counterculture, feminism, drugs, free sex, and protests against the war, second wavers had more resiliency by virtue of being youthful teenagers. As Gottlieb says, "It was simply their environment, and they swam in it like fish in the sea, adapting to its hazards and opportunities."[10]

What Gottlieb identifies as the first and second waves of the '60s, others have called the older boomers. Born between 1946 and 1954 the older boomers not only experienced the powerful events of the '60s, they also were the first to get their piece of the economic pie in the early '70s. *Business Month* identifies the older boomers as the group that "became prosperous quickly, grabbing the best jobs and getting in on the housing boom."[11]

The younger baby boomers, born between 1955 and 1964, who barely remember many of the startling events of the '60s, are far more likely to have faced disillusionment as a result of the downward mobility of baby boomers. Rather than facing social and political change, younger boomers have faced economic loss. The last good year for the middle class was 1973, when a thirty-year-old man could meet mortgage payments on a median-priced home with about a fifth of his wage. In the 1990s the same home is afforded by those who can pool their resources.

Sandra Tsing Loh in the *Los Angeles Times Magazine* reported that 36 percent of homes in the inflated Los Angeles market are bought by nontraditional homeowners. The majority of them are unmarried couples, followed by singles who put their money and incomes together to buy a house.[12] The rest are married persons who depend on both incomes to afford their dream house.

As boomers entered the '70s, the twin pillars of the middle-class dream—affordable housing and enough real income to support children—were still in reach. But by the late '80s and early '90s, inflation and rising interest rates had left most younger boomers behind. Katy Butler talks about her economic welfare compared to her parents:

> By the '80s, my parents had raised three children and achieved all of the American dream on my father's income alone—and after 15 years in the full-time work force, I could not afford a child and had never owned a new car. . . . Nowhere was the change more striking than in what each generation paid for housing and what they got for it. My parents paid $190 a month—on a 5 percent mortgage— for a four-bedroom house on an acre of land in Connecticut. Bob and I, with a combined income slightly lower than my father's paid $1,500 a month—on a 9 percent mortgage—for a five-room bungalow slightly larger than my parents' deck. Yet we felt lucky to afford a house at all.[13]

The problem for boomers is that their belief in the traditional values of home, marriage, family, and work has cost them dearly.[14] The American dream, portrayed through countless television programs as being the model home in the suburbs complete with a white picket fence and a two-car garage, is out of reach for most boomers. The sitcom family—a happy housewife at the beck and call of little Johnny and Becky and a husband who works in the "real world"—was (and is) a Hollywood illusion that pricks at the conscience of hardworking boomers of both sexes who wonder if they will ever "have it made."

Unfortunately, for many boomers, especially those born after 1954, buying a house and raising a family is still an impossible dream. To be able to do one of them would be an accomplishment, but to do both— to buy a home and raise a family—is beyond the ability of many in the baby boom generation. Rather than becoming homeowners, most Americans born between 1955 and 1964 seem doomed to rent. And with a 50 percent divorce rate, the family has become a revolving door of ever-changing relationships which never remain the same.

Ironically, the largest demographic group ever seen in America, 77 million strong, the group to whom parents held out such promise, is the same group who over the course of eleven years, from 1963 to 1974, would be most affected by the gut-wrenching events of those years, events that caused America to ask how much more it could take.

In contrast to the events baby boomers experienced as they grew up, a 1989 survey called "My Generation," published in *Seventeen*, helps put this in perspective. Polling teenagers ages fourteen to twenty-one—the group demographers call the baby bust, the group that follows the baby boom—the survey talked about the catastrophic events the baby bust generation had experienced in its lifetime. It stated:

In the world you have grown up in there have been catastrophic events: The President was shot and wounded; a space shuttle carrying a schoolteacher blew up before your very eyes; the Chernobyl nuclear plant spewed toxic radioactivity; the stock market crashed.

But there were also crises that happened gradually and not all-of-a-piece. Violent crime and drug abuse turned one city neighborhood after another into a danger zone. The homeless population soared. The greenhouse effect made us fearful about the future of the environment. The national deficit grew to astronomical proportions. And our opinion of public education took such a tumble that it's uncertain it will ever recover.[15]

To the calloused eyes of a baby boomer, especially an older boomer, who lived through the tumultuous years of the '60s, this sounds like nothing. Even the Gulf War in all its blood and glory did not shake a person's soul as did the experience of hearing that your heroes were murdered or that your best friend was missing in action or that your fiancé was blown up in Vietnam when he stepped on a land mine. For beyond the tragedies of the assassinations of political leaders and the economic and social upheaval of these years was the death of over 58,000 young Americans in Vietnam.[16]

The soldiers of Vietnam were the youngest to ever leave our shores. They fought and died at an average age of nineteen, seven years younger than those who served in World War II[17] and nine years younger than those who served in the Persian Gulf.[18] The ones who served in Vietnam were from the common stock of America, men like Joey Sintoni who grew up in Sagamore, Massachusetts. After joining the army, Joey served as part of the honor guard for funerals at Arlington National Cemetery. Realizing that the men who were dying in Vietnam were men his own age, he volunteered to serve in Vietnam. In January 1968 he was stationed in the Mekong Delta area near the Cambodian border. When he arrived, he unfurled a large American flag and attached it to a tank. After a few weeks of battle his flag, which he had brought with him from Arlington, was burnt up when the tank was hit by a rocket. Of the flag he wrote, "It flew proudly to its hot death."

Joey went to Vietnam with high expectations of fighting for a noble cause and of defending America. But after two months of battle, he was the only one of a group of twelve men who was alive or able to fight. In his diary he wrote:

I am not trying to be a fatalist, but I realize I'll never be able to make one year alive in the field, unless the fighting drastically changes or the war ends, both of which are unlikely. The "oldest" guy in my platoon, one still in the field, still able to fight, has been here six and a half months. All of a sudden I realize I may never see the woman or family my heart beats for. I dare not make a friend.[19]

Nineteen days later Joey was dead. Before his death, Joey wrote a letter to his girlfriend, Angela, which was to be delivered to her in case he died. His devotion to his country is expressed in these words:

Vietnam is a test of the American spirit. I hope I have helped in a little way to pass the test. The press, the television screen, the magazines are filled with the images of young men burning their draft cards to demonstrate their courage. Their rejection is of the ancient law that a male fights to protect his own people and his own land.

Does it take courage to flaunt the authorities and burn a draft card? Ask the men at Dak To, Con Tien, or Hill 875, they'll tell you how much courage it takes.

Most people never think of their freedom. . . . Why must people take their freedom for granted? Why can't they support the men who are trying to protect their lifeblood, freedom?

I've died as I've always hoped, protecting what I hold dear to my heart. We will meet again in the future. We will. I'll be waiting for that day.

The inevitable, well, the last one: I love you with all my heart and my love for you will survive into eternity.

Your Joey [20]

The story does not end there. Joey's death, like all the deaths in Vietnam, sent waves of grief and confusion through family and friends. After hearing the news of Joey's death, Angela's dreams for the future went up in smoke. They had already picked out the names for their children who would fill their two-story dream house overlooking the Cape Cod Canal. She said after Joey's death: "I lost that dream. When he died, I just didn't pick up the pieces and go out and find some boyfriend I could marry. . . . I was supposed to marry Joey Sintoni. I didn't find it easy to progress to Plan B. Marriage was killed in action."

Eight days after Joey died, Martin Luther King, Jr. was gunned down, and two months later Robert Kennedy was assassinated. Angela's world was on fire. Of her feelings she said: "I had that sense of futility, of what's the use. It took a long time for me to care again and feel hopeful. . . . It made me old real fast."[21]

The death of Joey was also the death of Angela's dreams, an experience shared by millions of baby boomers. The boomers who burned draft cards and protested in the streets did so not out of disrespect or because they were unpatriotic; they did so because they knew something was terribly wrong. The generation that as children had said the Pledge of Allegiance with eyes focused on the American flag in schoolhouses across America now questioned all that it stood for.

"I pledge allegiance to the flag of the United States of America." How could you pledge allegiance to a flag under whose banner your brothers, friends, and lovers were being slaughtered by the thousands in an undeclared war? "And to the republic for which it stands, one nation under God." What kind of God would bless this kind of war in which the most powerful nation on earth would send 2 million of its young into a war that it had no desire of winning and whose strategic importance rested on the so-called "domino theory"? "Indivisible, with liberty and justice for all" seemed to be a reality only for the wealthy and the white who could keep their sons out of Vietnam.

Some twenty years later baby boomers talk about the bitter disillusionment resulting from the war in Vietnam. *Rolling Stone,* in its "Portrait of a Generation" survey, reported that almost half of the baby boom generation have personal knowledge of the human losses in Vietnam. Forty-eight percent of them, 70 percent of them in their early forties, knew someone—a friend, relative, or acquaintance—who was killed, missing, or wounded in Vietnam.[22]

Vietnam vets have had an especially bitter pill to swallow. Many returning home from the war were vilified by their peers. Flashbacks, suicide, Agent Orange, and homelessness affect many. Anger, hate, frustration, and low self-esteem are the demons they have fought since coming home. Most vets felt abandoned by the ones they loved and by the country for which they had fought. They were the American warriors who were not welcomed home as heroes by their fellow Americans.

The one constant theme of the Gulf War was that "we" were not going to do it again. Regardless of how we felt about the war, the soldiers were not going to be abandoned or forgotten. So Americans unfurled their red, white, and blue flags and tied yellow ribbons around trees, houses, and buildings. They wore yellow bows on their blouses and suits as if they were a badge of honor. They sent videos, cards, cassette tapes, T-shirts, bubble gum, and brownies in shipments that flooded the military's capacity to carry them. They welcomed home the Gulf veterans with parades, speeches, and TV specials. All of this was done in a frenzy of activity that had more to do with unresolved guilt over Vietnam than with welcoming home the victors of the "One Hundred Hour War."

The most profound symbol and lasting remembrance of the '60s experience is a black granite, V-shaped wall with the names of 58,132 veterans who died in the Vietnam War. The uniqueness of the Vietnam Veterans Memorial lies not in its shape, but in the polished surface of the black granite in which you can see your own reflection wavering over the names of those who gave their lives in Vietnam.

In many ways it has become America's wailing wall. Since its dedication November 11, 1982, it has become the most visited monument in Washington, D.C. Laura Palmer, the author of a moving book about people's experiences and remembrances of Vietnam, *Shrapnel in the Heart,* said of its dedication:

> It was then that America finally turned to embrace her own. Engraved on the wall's black granite panels that pry open the earth are the names of every man and woman who went to Vietnam and never returned. In dedicating the memorial, America finally acknowledged that we lost more than the war in Vietnam; we lost the warriors. The war was deplorable, not the men who served.[23]

As the Vietnam Veterans Memorial is the lasting symbol of the events of the '60s, the resulting spiritual root of the baby boom generation is one of brokenness, a sense of loss and disillusionment over what happened to them and a clear break from the assumptions that guided their parents' generation. This sense of not being whole, of still trying to survive the turmoil of their youth, of living with unfulfilled expectations has produced three other spiritual realities in baby boomers: loneliness, rootlessness, and self-seeking, which play a part in the daily lives of the baby boom generation.

Chapter Two

LONELINESS

For almost two weeks I had been meeting daily with eight other pastors to share our needs and concerns about our families, the churches we served, and our relationships with other pastors. On the next to the last day, we came to realize that what bothered us most was the devastating feeling of loneliness that went with the job; the belief that no one could understand what it was like to be a pastor in a society that seemed no longer to need the church, to have to deal with the problems of church members without disclosing our own pain, to realize how afraid we were to be a friend to others in the fear that they would use our vulnerabilities against us.

Little did I realize that our group was not the only one that was feeling this way. Across America people who are compulsive shoppers, cancer patients, sex addicts, schizophrenics, and alcoholics have been gathering together in record numbers in support groups. In February 1990 it was reported that 15 million Americans gathered weekly in support of groups of one kind or another. This phenomenon is an indication of something very important: People want more out of their lives than just the daily grind of living; they long to have meaningful relationships. Commitment, marriage, and family are no longer bad words in the vocabulary of boomers. But how to find these things and where to find them requires sorting out what has happened in their personal lives since the '60s.

The question that arises from the success of support groups is, Why does there seem to be such a need to find someone like ourselves? Could it be that the popularity of support groups, especially to the baby boom generation, contains in it a clue about what truly ails the members of today's society? The success of support groups is not the only indicator that tells us that something has happened to the soul of the everyday American. When looking at baby boomers, we find the following facts, which shed light on the changing values and norms of American society.

Fifty percent of their marriages will end in divorce.[1]
Thirty percent have lived together outside of marriage.[2]
Fourteen percent were pregnant outside of marriage.
Five percent have had an abortion.[3]
Twenty-five percent of baby boomer women will remain childless.[4]
Twenty-five percent will only have one child.[5]
Thirty-three percent are single.
Sixteen percent are single parents.
Twenty-six percent of them are in marriages where both husband and wife work.[6]
Fewer than five percent live in a traditional marriage where the husband works and the wife stays home with the children.

Percentages don't tell the whole story. When we put these percentages into actual numbers, the facts are startling. When we say that 33 percent of baby boomers are single, we are talking about 25 million people born between 1946 and 1964. When we say that 30 percent have lived together outside of marriage, we are talking about 22 million Americans in this generation. When we say that only 5 percent live in a traditional marriage where the husband works and the wife stays home with the children, we are talking about 73 million out of 77 million baby boomers who do not live in a '50s style marriage, precisely at the age when their parents would have expected them to be married and settled down in a home with at least two children.

What used to be called a family no longer pertains. To a baby boomer a "family" could mean a number of options. A family could be a divorced man and a divorced woman living together in a trial marriage. A family could be a remarriage on the part of both husband and wife, each bringing along a couple of children, thus making a blended family. A family could be two homosexuals living together, or a single parent with two children. A family could be a baby boomer with two of her children living with her older parents, or it could be a single man, who has never been married, living alone. The descriptions of a family are endless.

In *The Postponed Generation,* Susan Littwin talks about Kathleen, a baby boomer who worked in her department at school. Kathleen had told her in the fall that she was going to take an accounting job with a "big eight" firm after Christmas. But Christmas went by and spring came, and Kathleen was still in the office. In a casual conversation Susan discovered that Kathleen had not moved on to the "big eight" because during the Christmas holidays she had gotten married.

Since Christmas, Susan and Kathleen had had innumerable conversations about all kinds of things but Kathleen had failed to mention that she had just married, something her mother would have proclaimed in headlines in the newspaper. When Susan asked her why she had failed to mention her marriage, Kathleen and she had the following conversation.

"I don't know," Kathleen says in her soft voice, pushing the hair out of her very lovely blue eyes. "I just didn't want people to think I had changed or to act different toward me. When you're married, people expect you to act out a certain role, and I don't want a role. I just want to be myself. For instance, my father thinks I ought to be buying furniture and china now that we're married. I have no interest in any of that right now."

"Why did you get married? " I asked.

"Well, I was in this relationship, and I didn't know where it was going. He's going east in the summer, and wanted me to come with him, so he said, 'Let's get married,' and we did. But it doesn't really make anything different." [7]

Kathleen's attitude toward marriage is very different from that of previous generations. When her parents' generation got married, it was a lifelong commitment, made in the belief that people should stay together "for better, for worse, for richer, for poorer, in sickness and in health, till death do us part." [8]

But since the '60s the emphasis of relationships is no longer focused on commitment and sticking it out no matter what. Instead we have Kathleen's remark: "I just want to be myself." In fact, for baby boomers like her, marriage is a controversial choice. For them the norm is to float in and out of a series of relationships which last as long as they work out. More tellingly, marriage for people like Kathleen is just one possible lifestyle option in a world of confusing, changing relationships.

The result of this wide-open lifestyle where choices are made for the moment is loneliness. When asked in a *Rolling Stone* survey, 23 percent of baby boomers said they were concerned about being lonely, about having no one to live with. [9] Robert Weiss, in his groundbreaking book *Loneliness: The Experience of Emotional and Social Isolation*, gives a similar answer, estimating that 25 percent of Americans regularly report suffering from loneliness. [10]

When Weiss did his work in 1973, he found that little research had been done on a subject that affects almost one in four Americans. He said, "Loneliness is much more often commented on by songwriters than by social scientists." [11] When considering why people were reluctant to talk about it, he found that it is "such a painful, frightening experience that people will do practically everything to avoid it."[12]

One writer who was going to a conference on loneliness was on an airplane when the woman sitting next to him asked him where he was going. After he told her he was going to a conference on loneliness, she blushed, stammered, and quietly said to him, "I'm sorry."

Many have this attitude about loneliness because they think it only affects people who are painfully shy, widowed, divorced, or unhappily single. But in fact people in these types of situations are more likely to feel lonesome than lonely. Loneliness is something that is much deeper than a temporary condition of being alone. Weiss says:

> Loneliness appears always to be a response to the absence of some particular type of relationship or, more accurately, a response to the absence of some particular relational provision. In many instances it is a response to the absence of the provisions of a close, indeed intimate, attachment.[13]

In other words, loneliness is the result of a breakdown of meaningful relationships. Just being with someone does not bring about a cure. Those who have been recently widowed or divorced oftentimes feel quite alone even though they are with a group of friends.

In order to understand loneliness we must first understand what it is to have a meaningful relationship. James Flanders, writing in *Loneliness: A Sourcebook of Current Theory, Research and Therapy*, develops what he calls a "Concept of Human Contact."[14] In his work he identifies seven essential features of human contact.

The first two features are (1) time for frequent interactions and (2) time for informal interactions free of pressing role demands.[15] Most of the time we interact with people on the basis of roles. At work we interact with the boss or the secretary or the customer. In the family we are the parent or child or husband or wife. At church we are the layperson or the pastor. Very few are the times when we interact with people outside of these role demands.

Relationships that have long-lasting meaning have a sense of serendipity to them, of playfulness and compassion rolled into one. This happens only through frequent interactions between people who are freed from playing a part in a scripted role of life.

While people may be aware of the need for time for these kinds of interactions, finding the time is becoming more difficult because of the increasing demands that are placed upon them. A Harris survey found that the average work week has grown six hours, from forty-one hours to nearly forty-seven since 1973.[16] This does not take into account the increasing number of hours per week it takes to commute to work, especially on the overcrowded freeways that plague big cities across the country.

Another study found that the loss of time between marriage partners because of the increasing demands of work took away from the activities couples found to be the most meaningful and satisfying in their marriages. Time spent together in activities such as eating, playing, and conversing proved to be much more fulfilling than time spent on activities such as child care, housework, watching television, or community service.[17]

Time is scarcer for women because married women who are employed full time come home to do a second shift. Arlie Hochschild, a sociologist at the University of California, Berkeley, found that working wives typically do 75 percent of the household chores around the house.[18] In a 1987 survey working women estimated that they did thirty hours a week of work around the house, while their husbands estimated they did four to six hours a week. Other studies have shown that working wives put in three times as many hours around the house as do their husbands.[19]

Although husbands have increased their time doing household chores from 20 percent in 1970 to 30 percent in 1990 and have increased their role in child care,[20] many women find this to be grossly unfair. Hochschild points out that many men are satisfied to have it both ways—a wife who brings home a paycheck and also does the chores at home.[21]

Boomers are not only strained for time in relation to husbands or wives or meaningful others; children and parents also make demands on their time. One of the most pressing concerns for boomers is how to take care of their parents who need more care and attention as they grow older. A report from the Older Women's League found that women can expect to spend seventeen years of their lives raising children and eighteen years helping an aging parent.[22]

More and more boomers are faced with the heartrending decision of how to take care of parents who can no longer live on their own. Should they bring parents into their own house, find a retirement home, or put them in a rest home? As boomers and their parents age, these are some of the hardest choices they will ever face.

As a result, many boomers find themselves caught in a web of demands from a variety of sources—from work to home, from children to parents, to friends and relatives, and on and on it goes. Is it any wonder that boomers do not have time to be involved in community activities? Seventy-seven percent say that it has been a change for the worse that they are not as involved in community activities as their parents were.[23] In spite of their collective guilt over this, a fair assessment of time would say that, for many, being involved outside of work and family is an almost impossible task.

Any group that seeks the help of baby boomers to do its work—whether it is the church, the Red Cross, or any community organization—needs to realize that boomers are far more likely to be willing to pay to get something done than to volunteer their time. Anyone who asks boomers to come to a meeting or an activity had better make sure it is worth their time or you will never see them again. Because boomers recognize how little time they have to develop meaningful and lasting relationships, their most important commodity is time, not money.

A third feature of human contact is self-disclosure,[24] the willingness and ability to share one's deepest feelings and emotions in a safe and trustworthy environment. Self-disclosure is something that develops over the length of a relationship. Sadly for baby boomers, they are more likely to have to buy this type of relationship than to find it in their daily interactions with people who are close to them. Sixty-three percent said they were more likely to use psychiatry as a means of solving their problems than their parents had been.[25] Some might rightly say that the previous generation had no lock on self-disclosure, but there is a sense in which boomers have lost connection with the people around them.

Baby boomers are far more likely to talk to a psychologist than to a friend, pastor, or family member about a problem they are experiencing. A number of them, at the least sign of trouble with a child, will take that child to a child psychologist to try to straighten things out. Earlier in our history the extended family provided an environment of trust where self-disclosure could happen. In the world of the baby boomer, self-disclosure takes place in the office of a psychologist or in the midst of a circle of strangers.

Part of the attraction of the support group is that one can reveal his or her deepest secrets to people with whom one does not have to deal on an everyday, personal basis. It is much safer to reveal ourselves in anonymity than to tell all to a loved one who really knows us and can confront us on a much deeper level in the midst of an ongoing relationship.

The fourth feature of human contact is touching.[26] We live in a world that is increasingly high-tech and low-touch. Instead of playing ball with a friend, children are more likely to play a Nintendo game in front of a TV monitor. People are increasingly being replaced by television, computers, and after-hours banking machines. Louise Bernikow, writer of *Alone in America: The Search for Companionship,* says,

> American life has become privatized. People are wrapped up in selfish, individual pursuits of material goods. We're not often encouraged to value people.
>
> We also live in a world where it's not so clear what other people are for any more. . . . All the advances in our life may not cause isolation, but they have made it more possible to live that way.[27]

In our fast-paced, win-at-any-cost, individualistic society, millions of people can go weeks at a time without a hug or the touch of a loved one. Monkeys in cages at the zoo give more attention to one another than many of us do in our daily lives. One of the saddest results of loneliness is that when people are out of contact with others they become one of the untouchables, not because of disease, but because they do not feel they have the permission to touch other people.

The fifth feature of human contact is the *favorable* exchange of resources, which must occur over months and years. This exchange has a value that cannot be found in any other way. Worth is found in the relationship itself. More important there is something special created because the people involved are willing to give of themselves to the other person. They are willing to invest in the other what is most precious to themselves—their time and attention.[28]

A century ago marriage offered a number of resources that were in high demand. First, there was the sexual relationship between husband and wife. Even though a husband might visit the local bordello, the double standard ensured that a woman did not play around. Second was the economic necessity of teaming up: The husband took care of the work outside the home, and the wife took care of the children and the housework. Third, the clearcut roles of husband and wife made it socially unacceptable to be unmarried. Society demanded marriage as a moral absolute. To be unattached was to live outside the norms of civilized society.

For baby boomers things are much different than for previous generations. Today's norms are much more permissive than norms of the past. As a result, society has made it possible to have sexual needs satisfied by a number of different partners. Men and women alike have the freedom to experiment. Society's standards have changed so rapidly in the last twenty years that any kind of behavior and lifestyle seems to be acceptable as long as it is "safe."

Even though boomers have grown up as part of the sexual revolution, 59 percent of baby boomers said that the more permissive attitude of their generation about sex was a bad thing, and 53 percent regarded the increased openness toward homosexuality as a step back from where their parents' attitude had been.[29]

But even this shows how much things have changed. When these questions were asked by *Rolling Stone*, the questions were framed to get a response of worse or better. The words *worse* or *better* reflect an unwillingness to distinguish between right or wrong. For example, a hamburger at McDonald's might be better or worse than one at Burger King, but both are all right, depending on your choice. No one would say that it was wrong for Burger King to cook a hamburger, and no one seems to be willing to say whether a particular lifestyle is right or wrong.

Things have changed in the economic sphere as well. Women today are able to sustain themselves economically outside of marriage, although boomers will tell you it takes two checks to live the American dream.

If sexual and economic needs can be met on an individual basis and if any lifestyle is acceptable, what scarce commodity do people have to offer to one another in today's world? The answer is companionship—not love, not money, not sex, not material goods, but spending quality time with a person over weeks, months, and years. For baby boomers the scarce commodity that they are looking for is not someone who will sleep with them but someone who will stay with them even in their darkest hours.

The sixth feature of human contact that brings with it a lasting relationship, is a *fair* exchange of responsibilities between both parties. More than talking about equality in relationships, this refers to how much each person is willing to invest and to give to the other person. This is especially important in the raising of children. To maintain strong and resilient ties with a child, parents must give at considerable cost to themselves. One of the stark realities of divorce, which will affect half of the marriages of baby boomers, is what happens in the relationship between children of divorce and their fathers.

Suzanne M. Bianchi and Judith A. Seltzer, in an *American Demographics* article, "Life without Father," said: "Mom and Dad are divorced. Dad drops by on Saturdays to take the kids to the zoo. This stereotypical image softens the harsh realities of divorce. But most of the children of divorced parents must live with the realities. Over half see their absent parents (nine out of ten times their father) less than once a month. One-third never see their father."[30]

In my church work I come into contact with these children all the time. I call them the "shuttle kids" because they are moved from parent to parent on different weekends and holidays, depending on whose turn it is to have them. Many times I get the impression that the parent who gets them has won the booby prize for that weekend. The effects on children in these situations can be very damaging to their self-esteem. Although they may seem to be thick-skinned survivors who can take on the world, many of them in private will confess to a deep longing for continuity and lasting love. Many will admit to feeling very lonely.

Not only do children feel the effects of this separation, and this coming-and-going lifestyle, the long-term implications for parents who do not see their children is frightening. Thirty years down the road, who is going to take care of the fathers and mothers who failed to see their children when they were young? Who will be the caregivers to the millions of single elderly who elected not to have children or who have become estranged from their children as a result of divorce and separation? What child who was abandoned at age six will want to see the father when he's seventy-five?

Cheryl Russell wrote in *100 Predictions for the Baby Boom* that the decisions boomers make today will affect what their lives will be like in the future. The happiness of baby boomers in their old age hinges on two things, "children and money." Of children she says,

> Unfortunately, most Americans believe the myth that parents cannot count on their children in old age. Because American society has been so slow to adjust to the new rules of economic life, it is doubly hard for the baby boom to make the best long-term investment that it can make—the investment in children.[31]

Because boomers focus on short-term rewards, they fail to see the long-term results of their unwillingness to invest in relationships. If your outlook is constantly "What's in it for me?" it is hard to understand what reciprocal benefits you can get from a relationship that seems to be going nowhere. The catch is that enduring family partnerships require considerable personal cost and work. Marriages do not just happen. After the bliss of the honeymoon comes a time of learning to live together. Parenting is not automatic. It takes commitment and endurance to raise a child. It takes patience to wait for the long-term rewards of building lasting relationships, patience which many boomers have not learned to develop.

The seventh factor in developing human contact that leads to long-lasting relationships is a feeling of closeness. Flanders says that the biggest block to developing closeness is the raising of expectations that other people are not able to fulfill.[32] One characteristic of baby boomers that leads to loneliness is their high expectations, which are very hard to meet. Raised in an era of economic growth and abundance, they have come to expect a lot out of life.

Susan Littwin, who told us about Kathleen, the young woman who did not want to admit that she was married, says that beyond expectations many baby boomers live with a sense of entitlement. Like the children of the very rich, middle-class children raised in the '60s exhibit much of the same attitude.

> They put a great emphasis on the self, dislike answering to others, believe that things will somehow work out for the best, that their fantasies will come true, and that the world they move in will be strung with safety nets. . . . Many middle-class young people add special expectations of their own to this already heady brew. Some of them feel entitled to good times, expensive equipment, and the kind of homes they grew up in. Others believe their rights include instant status, important, meaningful work, and an unspoiled environment.
>
> All of them believed that they had limitless choices, arrayed like cereals on the market shelves.[33]

Unlike their parents, who were raised in the Depression years and learned to sacrifice and save for the future, baby boomers want instant gratification. As one mother of a baby boomer told me, "My daughter wants all the nice things for her house now. She doesn't want to wait." It is no wonder that younger credit card holders, in their late twenties and early thirties, owe more money than any other age group.[34] Katy Butler, a boomer who writes about "The Great Boomer Depression," talks about her friend Roger and his wife who seemed to have it made—a fancy apartment, vacations throughout the world, and prestigious jobs.

> Recently, Roger explained the secret of their success: they were $18,000 in credit-card debt and he was leaving his nonprofit job for better-paying but more boring work in the computer industry to pay it off. "We both had grown-up jobs for the first time, and we thought we should be able to live like grown-ups," he said. . . . "I wanted to be able to pick up the tab for ten people, or take a cab when I wanted. I thought that part of being an adult was being able to go to a restaurant, look at the menu, and go in if you like the food, not because you're looking at the prices. . . . We have nothing to show for it. We were in a lot of denial, and finally the denial broke."[35]

As boomers face the problem of unfulfilled expectations in their economic life, even more unsettling are their unmet expectations in their personal lives. Raised on a steady diet of TV sitcoms in which problems were solved with a slogan and a laugh within thirty minutes, the immediacy of ongoing problems nags at what they thought life was supposed to be.

One young baby boomer remembers being told how wonderful she and her classmates were by their teachers at school. "After the first moon landing, our teacher told us that we were God's children, and that the world was ours."[36] The problem with this mentality is that if you come to believe that the world is yours, it is hard to understand why your spouse would rather watch a football game than engage you in a conversation.

As boomers struggle to find some closure in their relationships, to have a feeling of closeness with another human being, they continually fight the image of the perfect marriage, the perfect family, and the perfect lover, which no one this side of heaven will be able to live up to. Martin E. P. Seligman in an article on "Boomer Blues" says,

> Married partners once settled for duty, but today's mates expect to be ecstatic lovers, intellectual colleagues and partners in tennis and water sports. We even expect our partners to be loving parents. . . . It's as if some idiot raised the ante on what it takes to be a normal human being. We blindly accept this rush of rising expectations for the self. What's remarkable is not that we fail on some but that we achieve so many.[37]

In *Living Together, Feeling Alone*, Dr. Dan Kiley has identified a type of loneliness he calls "Living Together Loneliness."[38] This type of loneliness, which he distinguishes from uncoupled loneliness, primarily affects women in their thirties and early forties who are either married or living together with a man. He estimates there could be as many as 10 to 20 million women suffering from this kind of loneliness.[39] The women he identifies as having this problem are primarily baby boomers. Kiley writes:

> In my viewpoint, Living Together Loneliness has emerged as a problem only within the past twenty years. To understand my sense of psychological history, you must recall the definition of clinical loneliness as: a person's emotional response to a perceived discrepancy between expected and achieved social contact.
>
> The key word in this definition is "expected." Fifty years ago, most of our grandmas didn't expect their men to give them intimacy, sharing, and emotional belonging. This doesn't mean that they didn't want it or need it; they simply didn't expect it. They may have

been disappointed or sad, but without the expectation for closeness, they didn't experience the very private emotion of loneliness.[40]

Living together loneliness is primarily experienced by women in their thirties and early forties who are married but who feel that their man has let them down. Because loneliness is associated with being alone, they don't identify loneliness as being their problem. Instead, the problem seems to be with their husband or lover who does not pay them enough attention, is always too busy to talk to them, or ignores their needs. As their loneliness increases, they go through the stages of bewilderment, isolation, agitation, depression, and finally exhaustion.[41]

Unmet expectations also affect boomers in their work. I know of one extremely successful businessman who "has it made." Everything he touches turns to gold, but he never can seem to get enough. He is estranged from his wife and children. He has all the wealth in the world. But now that he has made it he asks, "Is that all there is?"

A highly successful accountant gave me this analogy to his life. He said that his career has been like scaling a cliff. When he graduated from college, he and his friends and family started together at the bottom of the cliff, taking the first steps up together. When they got to a rough spot, he would reach over to help them up. As he got higher and higher, the cliff got more treacherous and narrow. So instead of reaching down to help others, he found himself scratching and clawing his way over the backs of those ahead of him. Finally, after years of struggle and fighting his way up, he made it to the top only to find himself all alone. As he looked over the edge of the cliff, he could see his wife, children, and friends dashed against the rocks at the bottom of the cliff. He had made it to the top, but it had cost him all the people he had loved. Now at the age of forty-five, he wonders if there is any more to life.

Mid-career women who gave up having children for work often feel bitter about a business world that did not allow them the freedom to have both. Many of these women have been pioneers in the feminist movement who had to fight their way into male-dominated professions. They wonder if it is fair that 90 percent of male executives ages forty and under are fathers, while only 35 percent of their female counterparts are mothers. Elizabeth Mehren, 42, a feature writer for the *Los Angeles Times*, acknowledges that her generation believed they could control their biological clocks, but now time is running out and they have discovered they cannot control infertility. They are the ones who are making the ultimate sacrifice of having no children.[42]

As boomers are caught in the trap of rising expectations which never seem to be met, they find themselves in a state of emotional isolation. Cut off from meaningful and lasting relationships, millions of boomers are what they never expected to be—lonely. Kiley says this problem is fundamentally a spiritual problem.

> Because a lonely feeling is such a subjective experience, and almost never replicates itself, it's impossible to measure loneliness objectively. Consequently, the treatment program must involve some degree of spirituality; that is, asking a person to search for greater meaning in his or her life.[43]

Instead of searching for greater spiritual meaning in life, most lonely people find themselves trying to escape from their feelings and thus live a lifestyle that is characterized by rootlessness. What Weiss identifies as social isolation,[44] boomers experience as a constant search for something that will make them happy, something that will give them a lift, something that will make them feel satisfied. As if that is not enough, as baby boomers come to a point in their lives when they will make decisions that will affect all of society, they face a rapidly changing world where the old rules of politics, economics, and morality do not work any more. What boomers hoped for in the '60s—a chance to change the world—they will inherit in the '90s and the beginning of the next century as they face a world that is catching up to America and a world that is in a constant state of flux. To that constantly changing world and its resulting loss of stability we now turn.

Chapter Three

Rootlessness

In the summer of 1973 I was one of over 800,000 boomers who traveled to Europe. Unlike most who went traveling on their own, I went the safe way, on a tour with a Latin club. I remember the comical scene in the airport when it dawned on me that I was to spend my six-week discovery trip with about thirty-four retired Latin teachers and seven fellow boomers. Secretly I think my parents were relieved to see what good supervision I would be under, as this was my first major trip away from home. It was also good for my biceps, as I spent much of the time carrying bags for these older adults.

One scene from that trip stands out in my mind. We were riding in a tour bus past the center of Amsterdam when the tour guide pointed out "Hippie Square" where hundreds of hippies dressed in the garb of flower children were sitting and smoking marijuana. Raised in a conservative home, I had never seen a group of real hippies, except at the Tournament of Roses Parade, but that was no big deal, because everyone acted strange on New Year's Day in Pasadena. But here in Amsterdam was a group of people from my own country who seemed to come from a far different place than I did. Far from being fellow citizens, they looked as if they came from another planet. Yet these American youth were part of a great migration that was taking place in the late '60s and early '70s.

Annie Gottlieb in *Do You Believe in Magic?* describes the feeling of those who were on the move at that time.

That urge for wholeness would drive us to discover and embrace everything our own culture had put down or ruled out. The children of security, we hankered for risk. Children of the "nice," the reasonable and rational, we wanted vision, passion, pain. Children of technology, we longed to get our hands in the dirt. Children of Lysol, Listerine, and Wonder Bread, we were starved for texture, taste, and smell. It was all "out there," outside those sterile space colonies, the suburbs; on the road, on the land, among people who had nothing much but life itself.[1]

The boomers I saw in Amsterdam were just the tip of the iceberg. In the late '60s and early '70s millions of baby boomers were dropping out of traditional American society. Sporting long hair and love beads, they became part of the movement that wanted no part of the establishment. They hitchhiked on streets and freeways. They bought a Eurail pass and traveled throughout Europe living in youth hostels. They bought Volkswagen vans and toured the world, going wherever they felt led. The one thing they did not do was to go where anyone wanted them to go; they had a mind and an agenda of their own.

Parents of baby boomers were very much aware of the rebellion of their children against the established rules and values of society. Midge Decter, a parent of baby boomers, wrote:

As children of this peculiar enlightened class, you were expected one day to be manning a more than proportional share of the positions of power and prestige in this society: you were to be its executives, its professionals, its artists and intellectuals, among its business and political leaders, you were to think its influential thoughts, tend its major institutions, and reap its highest rewards. . . .

Beneath these throbbing ambitions were all the ordinary—if you will, mundane—hopes that all parents harbor for their children: that you would grow up, come into your own, and with all due happiness and high spirit carry forward the normal human business of mating, home-building, and reproducing—replacing us, in other words, in the eternal human cycle.[2]

Boomers, who were fully aware of these unspoken expectations, thought there should be more to life than a nine-to-five job, a Buick in the garage, and a house on Elm Street. They wanted their lives to have meaning and purpose; if they could not have that, they at least wanted to enjoy life and have fun. They wanted to experience all the world had to offer; they wanted to go beyond the survivor mentality of Depression babies; they wanted to have it all.

Every belief, idea, and tradition was up for grabs. Whether it was belief in the Christian God or democracy or wearing a suit and tie to work, boomers were ready to replace it with Eastern religions, socialism, and bell-bottom jeans. The argument ran something like this: "Look at the mess you have made of the world. Nuclear arms, Vietnam, racial inequality, sexism, and pollution are destroying the world. Give us our chance. We can do it better."

The end result of this rebellion against the traditions and viewpoints of the past, was rootlessness, focusing on personal needs and wants without having a sense of history or traditional beliefs to give a person guidance. Boomers became divorced from the institutions that held society together in an attempt to make a more just and loving world, but found that they had to make new rules and regulations as they went along. So change was embraced with a vengeance without the safety net of faith, community, or common culture to catch people when they fell.

Many thought this would just be a phase that boomers went through as they lived their youthful years. However, rather than abating, rootlessness persists to this day. Whereas loneliness is born out of unmet needs in personal interactions, rootlessness has as its source unmet expectations in relationship to society as a whole.

One may wonder how it came about that a whole generation would come to feel as though it was different from the rest, that its perspectives and values were far more insightful than the views that had been handed down from previous generations. To understand how this happened, we have to take a step back into history to see that from the start, baby boomers were treated much differently from generations that had come before.

Before the 1950s, children went directly from childhood into adulthood; there was no distinct period from age 13 to age 21, which we now call the teenage years. A young person left childhood gradually and went into the working world. Only the lucky and the few continued their education. Before World War II, a person with a high-school education was considered to be trained and ready to take on responsibilities in the adult world of work.

But the '50s brought a turn of events. For the first time, blue-collar workers had enough earning power to live middle-class lives. Spurred on by postwar productivity and the expansion of the economy, unions had won great victories for their workers. In 1925, blue-collar workers in manufacturing industries had become the largest single occupational group in the United States. As a result of their numbers, the unions and the people they represented became the dominant political force in the '50s. In the economy of the '50s and '60s all a person needed to advance in American society into a middle-class lifestyle was a union card and a willingness to learn a skill in the manufacturing industries.[3]

As blue-collar workers lived middle-class lifestyles, they took on the values and the dreams of the middle class. In the '50s more than half of all Americans lived what is now called a traditional lifestyle, with the father working and the mother staying home with the children. A 1959 survey found that three-quarters of all American couples wanted traditional families of three or more children.[4] Because of blue-collar gains there was little difference between the lifestyles of the middle class and the working class. A middle-class person might have a bigger house or a deeper carpet than a blue-collar worker, but for the most part everyone had the same type of consumer items.[5]

The newfangled goods of the '50s and early '60s were durable items such as refrigerators, washing machines, cars, and televisions. While the middle class settled into a mundane lifestyle, which even the advertising industry found safe and dull,[6] blue-collar workers began feeling as though they finally had it made. Boomer parents were not afraid to tell their children that they had lived through a depression and a war to get what they had. It had taken them a lifetime to acquire the trappings of the American dream.

Although the earnings gap between professional or managerial workers and industrial workers had not changed much in the '50s, one of the great boasts of the time was that in the new suburbs, a plumber could live next to a professor and an electrician could live next to a doctor. There was virtually no difference in lifestyle between them: all could drive the same cars and live in the same houses.[7]

In the midst of plenty and apparent affluence for all, the consumer culture was born. The innocent purchase of a television allowed an array of uninvited guests to visit the living room of the American household. For the first time advertisers were able to penetrate into the homes of all classes of Americans throughout the country and encourage them to buy the goods that proved they had arrived. One of the groups marketers found to be the most profitable was the teaming numbers of babies and children that made up the baby boom. As Ken Dychwald says in *Age Wave*:

> When the boomers arrived, the diaper industry prospered. When they took their first steps, the shoe and photo industries skyrocketed. The baby-food industry, which had moved 270 million jars in 1940, ladled out enough strained meals to fill 1.5 billion jars a year by 1953. The boom kids created an insatiable demand for the sugarcoated cereals and toys hyped on Saturday-morning cartoon shows. Cowboy outfits, very popular with toddlers in the 1950s, rang up sales of $75 million per year. As the boomers suffered scraped knees and runny noses, a massive pediatric medical establishment arose, and Dr. Spock became a national figure.[8]

As these same children became teenagers, a new phenomenon took place: They became consumers. Born in a time of affluence, many did not have to work because they received an allowance. Instead of joining the work force right out of high school, they were encouraged by adoring parents to grab hold of another element of the American dream—the college education. With another four years to delay the responsibilities of adulthood, the boomer generation invented its own culture, the teen culture.

Now that teenagers had money and time, they became a distinct group in American society. To the business world they became a market to whom goods could be sold. Teen clothes, teen movies, teen music, and teen fads became the rage. Although American teenagers were divided by class and race, marketing firms did their best to promote a universal teen identity.

As American adults labored for dull durable products, teenagers bought goods that were exciting and flashy. With the focus on their needs and wants, companies fell all over themselves to supply teens with their every need and desire—for a good reason: It was immensely profitable. By 1955 teenagers were purchasing 43 percent of all records, 44 percent of all cameras, 39 percent of all radios, 9 percent of all new cars, and an unbelievable 53 percent of all movie tickets. By 1959, the amount of money spent on teenagers by themselves and by their parents had reached a staggering total of $10 billion a year.[9]

As boomers developed their own cultural awareness, they turned to those who were most like them to develop their values and belief systems. As a result, those who had the greatest influence over this generation were not the teachers, the preachers, the government, or even their parents. The leaders of the youth culture came from an unexpected source, from the American lower class and from working-class England. Elvis Presley, the Beatles, the Doors, the Rolling Stones, the Supremes, and Bob Dylan were not the kids you would meet down the block in a nice middle-class neighborhood. Far from having the boyish charm of Wally in *Leave It to Beaver*, the rock stars who became the trendsetters for the young were more apt to spring from the night-mares of parents who held middle-class values so dear. For beyond the homogenized picture of America portrayed on television was the flip side of American culture heard on the radio. Charles Kaiser in *1968 in America* says:

> TV was a white medium, the one you turned on in your living room to watch *Leave It to Beaver* or *Father Knows Best*, family entertain-ment that reinforced the middle-class ideal of the white suburban family. With the mass production of transistors in the late fifties, radio became the medium you could enjoy anywhere, alone, out-doors, or under the covers (even after you were supposed to be asleep). What you heard put you squarely inside a world of your own,

a world just as subversive as the Frank Sinatra generation feared it might be—the raucous, untamed, black and white world of Little Richard, Elvis Presley, Jerry Lee Lewis, Buddy Holly, the jitterbug, and Murray the K.[10]

The message of rock 'n' roll had little to do with discipline, achievement, and professional careers. It was more apt to put down academics ("Another Brick in the Wall," Pink Floyd), to belittle the rigors of hard work ("Working in the Coal Mine," Lee Dorsey), or to mock authority ("Whoopee, We're All Going to Die," Country Joe & the Fish at Woodstock).

By 1965 a form of music that had been concerned with love and dancing began to convey three unmistakable messages. The first message was anger and hopelessness as seen in P. F. Sloan's "Eve of Destruction." Released in August 1965 it reached the top of the charts in five weeks and was labeled the fastest-rising song in rock history. Unlike songs by the Beatles, whose songs rose on the charts because of the group's popularity, "Eve of Destruction" became popular because of its message.

Its frightening words were accompanied by a pounding drumbeat that signaled that the end was near. In the decade-long history of rock 'n' roll, this song was the first to dredge up the fears of the boomer generation. Not only did it challenge the assumptions of the war in Vietnam, but it also invoked images of coming atomic apocalypse with words evoking the horrible scene of a world turned into a graveyard.

This was the first of a number of songs that would pound home the truth that boomers lived in a precarious world that could be blown up at any minute and in which they could lose their life at the whim and mercy of those in the "establishment." After all, it was their parents' generation that invented the bomb and put them at risk. It was their parents' generation that got them into war and asked them to defend their way of life, a way of life that boomers were not so sure they wanted to live.

The second message that echoed the boomers' growing discontent came from another 1965 number one hit, the Rolling Stones' defiant "Satisfaction." The verses, which were a parody of the banality of radio, TV, and advertising, were far outshone by the chorus, which boldly proclaimed to anyone who was listening that no one was going to stop this generation from getting whatever it wanted. In *The Sixties*, Todd Gitlin noted, "'Satisfaction' was a cross-yelp of resentment that could appeal to waitresses and mechanics and students, all stomping in unison."[11]

Beyond the themes of hopelessness and unfulfilled desires was a third theme: the hope of transcendence as exemplified by another 1965 hit, Bob Dylan's "Mr. Tambourine Man." Dylan, who had written "Blowing in the Wind," an anti-war anthem, offered to the youth of America an escape from the harsh realities of life into a transcendent state of peace and love.[12] The layered lyrics of this song moved a person into a different state of consciousness. Hearing it was not enough. What many desired was a total experience that captivated the soul and moved you to a different plane.

Many tried to enhance this experience with drugs. Gitlin, who was part of the movement at the time, reflects that "Mr. Tambourine Man" went down especially well with marijuana, just then making its way into dissident campus circles. "People began to hear that in order to understand this and other songs, one had to smoke marijuana. Many believed that to be part of the youth culture, they had to get high. Lyrics became more elaborate, compressed, and obscure, images more gnarled, the total effect nonlinear, translinear. Without grass, you were an outsider looking in."[13] Many early experimenters saw drugs as a way to find themselves and to see beyond the boundaries of the physical self. Like ancient mystics from the East or Native Americans sharing a peace pipe, they made it a ritual of communion with the universe. Wynston Jones, a screenwriter says, "Drugs and the Sixties increased my tolerance for ambiguity; there is no one reality."[14] When Paul McCartney tried marijuana for the first time during a gathering between the Beatles and Dylan, he was heard to say, "I'm thinking for the first time, really thinking."[15]

LSD was taken because it was considered to be mind-expanding. Some took it as a religious rite. In Gottlieb's book, Cherel Ito says, "The friend who gave it to me dressed me in white and sat me down in front of Buddha and read me the Tibetan Book of the Dead. I was at Filmore East."

Another boomer remembers that "somebody just came up to me and said, 'Are you searching?' I said, 'Yeah.' He said, 'Here's something to help you.' And he put it in my mouth. I kept it in there, and I was very happy I did. Because it gave me the vision and the courage to actually go after what I had been longing for my whole life, and that was a spiritual quest."[16]

This ideal of LSD as a wonder drug that would help America move into a new age of freedom and love had become the grounding for the counterculture movement as exemplified in the Haight-Ashbury district in San Francisco. On January 12, 1967, Allen Cohen held a press conference in which he announced there was going to be a Human Be-In in San Francisco. Boldly he announced:

> Now in the evolving generation of America's young the humanization of the American man and woman can begin in joy and embrace without fear, dogma, suspicion, or dialectical righteousness. A new concert of human relations being developed within the youthful underground must emerge, become conscious, and be shared so that a revolution of form can be filled with a Renaissance of compassion, awareness and love in the Revelation of the unity of all mankind.[17]

As the "be-in" started on January 14, Stanley Owsley, the pioneer of LSD production techniques whom the *Los Angeles Times* recognized as the "LSD millionaire," handed out free samples of his newest LSD product, White Lightning. A few months earlier on October 6, 1966, possessing LSD had become a misdemeanor, and selling it became a felony in California.[18] Now that it was illegal, it was even more of a turn-on. The "be-in" turned out to be the biggest acid party ever held and, in the eyes of its promoters, it was a grand success.

Over 20,000 people participated, and the news media saw it as evidence of an unexplained, unforeseen mass movement. More than anything, its mysteriousness was what attracted attention. It had Hindu, Buddhist, and Native American trappings. An astrologer had picked the date of the event. Even the Hell's Angels had played a part by volunteering to protect the sound equipment.[19]

To experts it was a confounding puzzle of drugs, politics, Eastern mysticism, and culture, which was in complete opposition to the values of traditional American society. The predominant question of the time was, "Why?" Why would these youth, who had been given all the opportunities that a modern, educated, and affluent society had to offer, want to follow Timothy Leary's slogans of "Tune in, turn on, drop out" and "Get out of your mind and into your senses"?[20] Driven by a curious mixture of fear and wonder, the news media did their best to cover the new hippie culture. Gitlin states:

> Thanks to modern mass media, and to drugs—perhaps the most potent form of mass communication—notions which had been the currency of tiny groups were percolating through the vast demographics of the baby boom. *Life, Time,* and the trendspotters of the evening news outdid themselves trumpeting the new youth culture. As with the beats, cultural panic spread the news, the image of hippiehood. . . . There was enormous anxiety about whether the

prevailing culture could hold the young; and on the liberal side, anxiety about whether it deserved to. It became easy to imagine that the whole of youth was regressing, or evolving, into—what? Barbarism? A new society into itself, a Woodstock Nation? A children's crusade? A subversive army? A revolutionary class? Astonishingly soon, Governor George Wallace and Dr. Timothy Leary agreed that what was at stake was nothing less than Western Civilization, the only question being whether its demise was auspicious.[21]

The Beatles added to the growing controversy about the direction the youth culture was going when the group graduated from marijuana to LSD and started writing music while high. During a tripped out session, Ringo Starr composed "Yellow Submarine."[22]

Later, when the Beatles released the album *Sergeant Pepper's Lonely Hearts Club Band*, it was immediately hailed by critics as the best album ever, while in the same breath, it was criticized for its alleged references to drugs. "A Day in My Life" was banned in England because Paul McCartney's lyric sounded as though he was getting high. Other songs got an equally negative review.

The song that generated the most controversy was "Lucy in the Sky with Diamonds," which sounded like something penned during an acid trip. People immediately thought that "Lucy in the Sky with Diamonds" was an anagram for LSD, but John Lennon contended it was only an accident and that this phrase was one his mother had used to describe a drawing of her he had made in school one day.[23] Peter Brown, who was the executive director of the Beatles' management company, says,

> *Sergeant Pepper* became . . . the album that most perfectly personified the incense-laden, rainbow-colored, psychedelic sixties themselves. With *Sergeant Pepper*, the Beatles ascended from pop heroes to avatars and prophets. The album was praised and dissected and studied like the Torah or the Koran.[24]

As the Beatles went, so did a whole generation. Thirty-five million baby boomers, or 46 percent of them, say they have used drugs. Seventeen million, or 23 percent, still do.[25] It is doubtful that any other product had as much market penetration as marijuana and LSD did in the '60s. Like the music, these drugs cut across all class lines, from the student in college, to the construction worker on the job, to the soldier in Vietnam.

Beyond drugs, which a slight majority say they have not used, what united the whole baby boomer generation as none other before or since was the music and its message. To find out what boomers were thinking or believing, you only had to turn on the radio. When I gathered with my friends, it was not unusual for us to sing songs accompanied by a guitar. "Where Have All the Flowers Gone?" and "If I Had a Hammer" were songs that expressed our heart language about life. Our source of spirituality was found in the music, *our* music, not in the Bible or the beliefs of the adult society. Terri Hemmert, a baby boomer disk jockey in Chicago, talks about what it was like at the time.

Rock was something universal, something you understood. If you went to California to visit relatives, the kids in California knew the same songs. Your parents didn't. Maybe it was something tribal—but it was real exciting stuff.[26]

But by the early '70s something went wrong with the pop culture of the youth. The Vietnam War was grinding to an end; the counter-culture was losing its impetus; the student movement was losing its cause; and the results of the high life were coming in. After the crowning achievement of mass psychedelic gatherings took place at Woodstock on August 15, 1969, the end of the movement began on December 6, 1969, at the Altamont Raceway near San Francisco at a Rolling Stones concert. Charles Perry says of the event, "In its way, it was the topper of all the giant rock festivals, because it was the end of the series. The nasty atmosphere of panic and hostility near the stage made it the symbolic dead end of a generation's adventure. At the concert a black man, Meredith Hunter, was killed and countless others severely beaten."[27]

By this time Haight-Ashbury had moved from pot and LSD to speed, hash, heroin, and cocaine. Instead of a place of idealism, it had degenerated into a cesspool of greed, violence, and paranoia. In the first seven months of 1970, there were fourteen drug-induced murders.[28]

In the fall of 1970, Jimi Hendrix and Janis Joplin dropped dead of drug overdoses. A few months later Jim Morrison collapsed and died, perhaps of drugs. All three were twenty-seven. In the same year the Beatles broke up, and in 1971 John Lennon proclaimed, "The Dream Is Over."[29]

So as boomers entered the '70s they found to their surprise that they were not quite as unified as they thought. Expecting to be welcomed by the working world with open arms, they found they were at a disadvantage because of the sheer size of their numbers. They were the most educated generation America had ever seen. Eighty-five percent finished high school, 50 percent attended college, 25 graduated, and 7 percent went on to graduate school. This compares to their parents' generation of whom 50 percent were high school graduates and 10 percent finished college.

Yet when they graduated from college, many were in for a rude shock. Of the 8 million college graduates who entered the work force from 1969 to 1976, which was twice the number of the preceding seven years, 27 percent or 2.1 million were forced to take jobs they had not been trained for—or were unable to find work at all.[30]

Many of those who found themselves not welcome in the work force were those who were the most idealistic. Instead of concentrating on science, business, or engineering, they studied social science, history or romance languages, which were the heart of a liberal arts major. Many of these same people went into the helping professions such as teaching, social work, church work, and nursing. Samantha Harrison, a thirty-two-year-old baby boomer who recently went back to college to get a master's in business said, "The last two taxi drivers I had were Ph.D.'s in liberal arts." Talking about her friends, she said:

> More and more young women are abandoning teaching, social work, nursing, for business. That's where the money is. . . . The people I hang out with are all over thirty. With liberal arts backgrounds. We talk about what we're gonna do when we grow up, when we get out of business school. It's a change of life in a way, being here. We've formed a Renaissance Club, yakkin' about Shakespeare, theater, books, politics. We don't want to become these little number-crunching automatons.[31]

Harrison and her friends are what Peter Kim, the senior vice president for research at J. Walter Thompson, calls, "Would Be's." They constitute the largest portion of the educated baby boomers who in spite of their education find themselves with low income. They are heavy into contemporary lifestyles and tend to be liberal. They are called would-be's because they are the part of the middle class who are facing downward mobility, and as a result they are the poor cousins of the yuppies.

Yuppies, who became the proverbial image of the baby boom in the mid-1980s, tend to be younger baby boomers who have hit it big in the business world. Yuppies are found in professional and managerial positions and are seen as the leading trendsetters for their generation. They are the people featured in TV shows such as *L.A. Law*. Tough, aggressive, and highly successful in their careers, they are the ones who former '60s activists say have sold out to the establishment.

Katy Butler talks of her feelings about herself in relation to the successful portrait of the yuppies: "Meanwhile, the newspapers were full of stories about yuppies and blackened redfish and new restaurants. The cognitive dissonance hurt my head: Was I the only one who felt like a failure? Was it only my friends who were in trouble?"[32]

This feeling of failure, of not making it, is the one thing that hurts would-be's the most. Caught between the altruistic beliefs of helping others and the economic necessity of making a living, they find themselves going back to school to be retrained, or changing jobs in rapid succession, or just giving up.

But even the yuppies find themselves in an unsettled position. After the stock market crash on Black Monday, October 19, 1987, Jack Maurer, an older baby boomer who makes his living on the Chicago Board of Trade, talked about the results of the crash to his fellow workers, most of whom were yuppies.

> Hey what's this gonna lead to? Lunchtime conversations have changed. They wonder about a cyclical depression. They wonder about their lifestyles. There's a lesson, important to all of us: it can happen. It means being born in the forties and fifties doesn't mean being born in an amusement park, where things are always wonderful. Generally, this is the way these white middle-class kids feel. In one day, they've discovered the world is a serious, potentially disruptive place. Nobody owes them a living. Nobody owes them luxury and good times. . . . They are beginning to realize the all-day joyride may be over.[33]

Walter Shapiro, in a 1991 article in *Time* called "The Birth and—Maybe—Death of Yuppiedom," gives a postmortem to the term that started in 1983 as a successor to *preppie* and summed up the fast-track living of boomers in the '80s. Now in the '90s it seems to have lost its validity because yuppies are souring on materialism and are looking for something else. But he warns us not to give up on them too fast, for although the term may have lost its glitter, there is still the taste of the good life on the lips of boomers who experienced it in the '80s.[34]

But yuppies, who have gotten most of the spotlight, make up only 8 percent of the boomer population. They are outnumbered by would-be's, who make up 20 percent of this generation. Two other economic groups, the elite workers (7 percent) and workers (65 percent) round out the economic profile of the generation. Elite workers are skilled workers who did not go to college or finish their college education but who have yuppie incomes because of their needed skills and inventiveness. They are what Kim calls "the silent majority of the affluent market."

The largest portion of the baby boom generation are workers.[35] Largely ignored in the public eye, they are the ones who are suffering the most from the loss of jobs in blue-collar work. Unlike their fathers who were secure in union jobs or who made a good living on the farm, they face an uncertain future. Peter Drucker, in *The New Realities*, gives us a view of the future of the blue-collar worker.

> In the early 1970s, industrial workers began to decline fast, first as a proportion of the work force, then in numbers, and finally in political power and influence. . . . By the year 2010 they will have shrunk in the developed non-Communist countries to where farmers are now, that is, to between 5 and 10 percent of the work force. . . .
>
> The less schooled will increasingly be seen by their more successful fellows, even by those who, like educated American blacks, are themselves members of a disadvantaged group, as failures, dropouts, as somehow "deficient," second-class citizens, "problems," and altogether inferior. The problem is not money. It is dignity.[36]

In *The Clustering of America*, Michael J. Weiss gives us a far different picture of American society from the one boomers were raised with in the '50s and '60s. Using the tools of demographics and marketing, he shows us how American society is divided into forty neighborhood types, called clusters, each with distinctive values, lifestyles, tastes, and consumer habits. Ranging from the blue-blood estates with million dollar houses, white-collar jobs, and tastes for Rolls-Royces and Jaguars; to public assistance where people live in poverty in inner-city ghettos, reside in government housing, and are more likely to ride a bus than drive a car, Weiss gives us a vivid portrait of the United States: a country that is far from being unified, where great inequalities exist, and where no one dominant culture prevails.

Within these forty neighborhood types are thirteen in which baby boomers make up the large majority. They are listed as follows from the richest to the poorest:

Young Influentials, ages 18-34, live in white suburbs, are college educated, and are mostly single and childless. What Kim calls yuppies. Comprise 8 percent of the baby boom population.

Young Suburbia, ages 24-44, live in upper-middle class housing in the outer suburbs, are college educated, and are the nesting ground for today's nuclear families. Comprise 14 percent of the baby boom population.

God's Country, ages 25-44, live in upscale, exurban boom towns, have moved away from the big city to work in high-tech companies in the country. The best educated cluster in America, they are the most mobile and solidly employed. Comprise 7 percent of the baby boom.

Blue-Chip Blues, ages 25-44, live in working-class suburbs, have high-school educations and work in blue-collar jobs. Having one of the highest concentrations of traditional families, they live in the blue-collar version of the American dream. Comprise 16 percent of the baby boom.

Bohemian Mix, ages 18-34, are concentrated in the nation's major harbor cities, which have nurtured the beatniks, the flower children, public-interest crusaders, and gays. Made up of blacks and whites, never-married and divorced singles, it is an eclectic mix of middle-class and poor. Comprise 3 percent of the baby boom.

Black Enterprise, ages 35-54, is the preferred term of address for many of the nation's black achievers who live in middle-class suburbs outside the urban core. Residents boast high education levels and work in white-collar jobs. Comprise 2 percent of the baby boom.

New Beginnings, ages 18-34, is the result of an adult population that is one-third single. They are highly mobile, live in apartments in middle-class neighborhoods, and work in white-collar jobs. Comprise 12 percent of the baby boom.

Blue-Collar Nursery, ages 25-44, is where young middle-class families first settle down in a landscape of recently built subdivisions and overcrowded schools. Mainly high-school educated, they work in blue-collar jobs. Comprise 6 percent of the baby boom.

New Homesteaders, ages 18-34, live in exurban middle-class boomtowns, have some college education, work in blue- and white-collar jobs, and have the highest concentration of military jobs. One of the fastest growing clusters, this group likes wide open spaces and is the poorer version of God's country. Comprise 11 percent of the baby boom.

Towns & Gowns, ages 18-34, is located around college campuses and is made up of alumni and students who are college educated and work in white-collar jobs. Comprise 3 percent of the baby boom.

Emergent Minorities, ages 18-34, live mostly in black working-class urban neighborhoods, made up of single-parent families. With some high-school education, they work in blue-collar and service occupations. Comprise 4 percent of the baby boom.

Single City Blues, ages 18-34, live in a poor man's bohemia. Made up of a mix of college-educated and high-school educated blacks and whites, they live in downscale city districts where they are united by their low salaries in blue- and white-collar occupations. Comprise 9 percent of the baby boom.

Hispanic Mix, ages 18-34, live in poor inner-city enclaves in multi-unit housing made up of predominantly Hispanic singles and families. They have grade-school educations and work in blue-collar or service jobs. Comprise 5 percent of the baby boom.[37]

Weiss's unique view of America is used by magazines to target audiences who would be most receptive to their message. Towns & Gowns people are far more likely to read *Modern Bride* than *Motorcyclist,* while someone in New Homesteaders would think a magazine about motorcycles would be great. *Reader's Digest* executives have begun to plan for the day when they will aim modified versions of the publication to different cluster groups. Readers in Blue-Collar Nursery will see ads for canned spaghetti, while Young Influentials will be reading blurbs about health spas and espresso makers. They may even tailor articles for different cluster groups according to their interests.[38]

Other industries try out new products in cluster groups. Have a new diaper? Go to the residents of Blue-Collar Nursery who have plenty of babies who need to be changed. Have a new microwave dinner? Try it out on the residents of New Beginnings who more often than not eat alone. Have a new social issue? Try it out on the politically savvy members of the Bohemian Mix who are always on the lookout for a new cause.

Looked at from a different perspective, the clustering of America shows us that baby boomers have lifestyles and needs that are quite diverse from one another. Some of them are like Dave and Kathy Boast, a couple who recently moved into the Ryan Estates in Paradise Valley outside of Phoenix, Arizona. Their move to the Ryan Estates was the fourth in the last seven years, which is a typical American pattern. Major life events such as marriage, having children, a job change, and divorce put people on the move.

Almost a fifth of all Americans relocate every year. Most people do so to move up the cluster ladder to more affluent communities. The Boasts reflect this pattern. "Even as we were building this house, we were already talking about how we wanted the next one to look. Most people around here stay two or three years and then move up. Our neighbors are always trying to better themselves through the size of their homes. They're constantly saying, 'We have 2,400 square feet but we really need 3,200.'"[39]

But the Boasts are not the typical boomers of the '90s. Instead of trying to get ahead, most are fortunate to stay even, and many are finding themselves moving down the cluster ladder instead of up.

Ralph Whitehead, a public service professor at the University of Massachusetts, has labeled one group of baby boomers as New-Collar Voters. Making up one-third of the baby boom, 25 million, they comprise nearly 15 percent of the electorate. Classified as a new breed of workers who embraces '60s style values, they tend to hold down jobs in the gray area between blue-collar laborers and white-collar professionals. They work as teachers, computer programmers, nurses, secretaries, and fast-food managers. They live in six clusters: New Homesteaders, Young Suburbia, Black Enterprise, Blue-Chip Blues, New Beginnings, and Blue-Collar Nursery. Calling them the "most deeply individualistic generation in human history," Whitehead says:

> What they have in common is that many accept the traditional values held by their blue-collar parents, such as commitment to home, family, and country. But they are more liberal than their parents on issues such as abortion, premarital sex, and marijuana use. And they're more tolerant of unconventional attitudes toward marriage and the changing roles of the sexes.[40]

Two other comments about this group of baby boomers are worth noting. Tom Kiley is a political pollster from Boston who credits the New Collar Voters for the election of his democratic candidate, Senator John Kerry. Kiley says:

> Their rootlessness reflects an overriding distrust of big government, corporations, and many public institutions—including traditional party politics. . . . While their parents learned from the Depression and the New Deal that government could be beneficial, their own experiences taught them to be skeptical. New collars are largely de-aligned or have never gotten aligned in the first place.

Lee Atwater, the young, hard-nosed Republican national chairman during the 1988 presidential race who helped bring in the boomer vote, died of cancer in 1991. As Atwater faced his death, he realized that what was missing in a lot of people's lives—compassion and love for others—was missing in his.[41] Of the New-Collar Voters, Atwater said:

> What I'm seeing is a new kind of trapped American in this age group. This generation was basically brought up at a time when there was

unprecedented optimism. But many voters are finding out for the first time that the American dream will not work out the way they thought it would.[42]

The one thing that stands clear about the baby boom generation is their rootlessness. Through a quirk in history they find themselves believing in traditional values but living nontraditional lives. They were raised in a youth culture where they were treated as equals, but because of their numbers they have found themselves competing against each other in the work force. Raised in a consumer culture that said, "You can have it all," they find themselves grabbing all they can before it runs out. Looking for transcendence through drugs, they have found that speed kills. Told that they were middle-class, they find themselves living in a nation divided into classes according to income, education, consumer tastes, and marriage patterns.

Ironically, instead of turning to one another for the values they hold in common, they have turned inward to themselves to find meaning and purpose. In the "Portrait of a Generation" survey done by *Rolling Stone*, this generation is described as one "that had retreated into itself" and as one that was "isolationalist."[43] The result of root-lessness is self-seeking: A person shuns the values of the outside world and looks inward to find meaning and purpose. What some have mis-takenly labeled as selfishness is instead an inner search for meaning and truth. It is to that search that we will now turn.

Chapter Four

SELF-SEEKING

In 1986 Whitney Houston hit the top of the charts with her number one song, "The Greatest Love of All," a soul-filled rock ballad that personified the credo of the '80s. The song is not about love in the traditional sense; it is not about romance between two lovers; it is not about God; it is not about brotherhood and sisterhood or giving to humanity. Instead, its message is that the greatest love is inside each person. The song, which portrays itself as a song of hope and love, holds within it a summation of the philosophy of the baby boomer generation: After the turmoil of the '60s and the disappointments of the '70s, the only thing that is going to bring meaning to life is learning to love yourself.

What some saw as greed, narcissism, and selfishness, boomers turned to as the natural result of brokenness, loneliness, and rootlessness. It wasn't that the baby boomer generation had given up on the world. Instead the baby boomer decided that the only person he or she could depend on was self. As Houston said, "Everybody's searching for a hero; people need someone to look up to. I never found anyone who fulfilled my needs; a lonely place to be and so I learned to depend on me."*

Baby boomers started coming to this conclusion in the late '60s and early '70s. As the counterculture, the rock stars of the '60s, and the student movement faded, this generation turned introspective. Now that the revolution was over, the present had to be filled with meaning. Many of the veterans of the various movements of the '60s found purpose in the human potential movement. Todd Gitlin says that all the encounter groups, therapies, and mystical disciplines were supposed to help people get down to their real selves. So people learned to "live in the present," to "go with the flow," to "give themselves permission," and to "get in touch with their feelings."[1]

This search for self happened in many unexpected places, and not everyone went through it willingly. I encountered it firsthand in my church youth group in the late '60s and early '70s. One time I remember being put in the middle of a circle and told to express my feelings about each person in the group. I really did not want to do it. I did not know what to say, but as it was the thing to do, I did it anyway. At another memorable meeting, I was taught to punch pillows to express my anger. It felt weird to be hitting pillows with my friends to express an anger I really did not feel. At a youth camp our pastor led us in a body awareness exercise where everyone laid on the floor in a line, side by side, and we took turns rolling over each other in an attempt to "find ourselves."

At that time it seemed as if everyone were on a search for something. Even the adults I knew were starting to do strange things. The parents of two of my friends decided to switch partners, so they divorced and married their newfound lovers. The most popular teacher at my high school divorced his wife with whom he had two children, and married one of the graduating seniors. Another friend was taken by his parents with his brother and two sisters to a nudist colony to experience nature. And his father was a pastor. The parents of another friend told me I was a medium and encouraged me to develop my psychic abilities. Another time I attended a meeting of a church member who interpreted our dreams and foretold our futures.

Baby boomers born after 1953 bore the brunt of this experimentation by adults. In school each teacher and school system decided to try new methods and techniques. Boomers went from new math to new English to open classrooms to schools without walls and so on. I always joke that I cannot spell because each year I was taught a new method. If it were not for "spell checkers" on computers, millions of baby boomers would not be able to write a sentence that doesn't have to be deciphered.

Dr. Judith Mack, the director of counseling at the University of California, Davis, in talking about younger baby boomers, commented that her most difficult, therapy-resistant cases came from homes where parents were so caught up in the changes in their own lives that they hardly had time to be parents. Their children were given every monetary advantage, when what they really needed were their parents.[2]

One boomer, now in her early thirties, remembered how her full-time professional mother suddenly lost interest in mothering and decided it was time to find herself. She says, "When I was in junior high, my mother got involved in art and causes. She took a studio and painted and had a lot of artist friends. She was also the head of a lot of committees. What I remember is that she was on the phone all the time."[3] Susan Littwin says:

> It is hard to remember how crazy all of that was. Couples are still divorcing and women, more than ever, are working and having lives outside of their families. But we have institutionalized the change and we go about our lives without guilt. There is day care and after-school care and family therapy and joint custody and dozens of other buffers that make it work routinely, if not painlessly. But in the sixties, the breakup of the nuclear family—with mamma at home—exploded on us.[4]

From 1966 to 1976 the divorce rate doubled from 2.5 per thousand to 5.0. The raw numbers went from 499,000 divorces a year in 1966 to 1,083,000 divorces in 1976. During the same period the marriage rate remained fairly stable, going from 9.5 in 1966 to 10.0 in 1976. Since then, the marriage and divorce rates have stayed fairly constant, at 10.0 for marriage and at 5.0 for divorce.[5]

By combining the figures of divorced single parents, which have grown dramatically from 694,000 in 1960 to 3,833,000 in 1988,[6] with a remarriage rate of 46 percent,[7] I estimated that between 1966 and 1976 about 17 million baby boomers went through a divorce with their parents. This would mean that 22 percent, or almost one in four baby boomers, have had parents who have gone through a divorce. Contrary to the image of boomers as persons who had a golden childhood, many boomers went through the emotional hardships that these changes brought about. The older boomers who were on the vanguard of social change stand in contrast to the younger boomers who bore the weight of these changes as seen in their family life and in their education at school.

When I perform weddings for baby boomers, I get a glimpse of what they face as a result of the breakup of their parents. About three-quarters of the weddings I perform contain two elements. First, the couple who is getting married has been living together. Sometimes one of them is divorced and has a child. The second element is divorced parents. It is interesting to see how couples handle these two elements. With respect to the first, the couple who has been living together thinks nothing of it. They do not see anything unusual in their pre-marital arrangement. They do not regard their lifestyle as sinful, which is what people in the '50s would surely have thought. What causes them embarrassment is their parents.

Invariably as we talk about the wedding ceremony, the question will come up, "What do I do about my parents?" A recent bride echoed the feelings of many boomers caught in this situation. "They're divorced, and my mother will be there with my stepfather, and my father will be there with his girlfriend. Where will they sit, and who should I ask to give me away? I think my father should give me away. But I've been raised by my mother and stepfather since I was about twelve, so I actually feel closer to my stepfather. But if he gives me away, my father will be hurt."

Questions such as these have nothing to do with etiquette. These questions have to do with processing what has happened in a family and trying to make sense out of what remains. One of my early experiences in ministry, in 1979, was helping a high-school senior deal with the divorce of her parents. Without warning, her mother left her father to go live with a boyfriend from work. This young boomer was angry, shocked, ashamed, and hurt all at the same time. I distinctly remember one of her remarks: "They both got lawyers, and last night they were fighting over who was going to keep an umbrella. Actually, it's my umbrella. As far as I'm concerned my mother can take the umbrella and shove it. I don't want it any more. I'll go get my own damn umbrella."

The relationship between boomers and their parents has a lot to do with self-seeking. Even the name of the '60s movement that causes the most soul-searching in the area of personal values and appearance— "the counterculture"—retained in it the element of adolescent rebellion against parental authority. After all, what good would it do to grow long hair if your parents did not complain about it?

Midge Decter, a mother of baby boomers, notes that boomers did things that were designed to provoke some kind of reaction from their parents. Raised as children in the middle class, boomers were expected to be well dressed; therefore, they "dressed themselves in rags." Raised with the expectation of being well groomed and healthy, they "cultivated the gaudiest show of slovenliness and the most unmistakable signs of sickliness." Raised on the premise that they would be prompt and well mannered, they "compounded a group style based on nothing so much as a certain weary, breathless vagueness and incompetence— enriched by the display of a deep, albeit soft spoken, disrespect for the sensibilities and concerns of others."

Directing her comments to boomers, Dector writes:

That key to this assertion of style lay in an exact reverse translation of what your parents had taken for granted on your behalf is only one mark of how necessary we were in all your efforts to define yourselves with the main issue for you so obviously being not "what in my own mature opinion will be best for me?" but "what will they think or how will they feel in the face of this present conduct of mine?"[8]

When I was in college, I drove my parents crazy by answering their question of what I wanted to do with my future by answering, "I'm just taking it one day at a time. God will take care of me." Yet the reality was that my parents were taking care of me—paying my tuition to college and providing for my housing, food, and car insurance. At that time it didn't dawn on me that their real qestion was, "When are you going to become an adult?"

There is an irony in all of this. Because their parents took such good care of them, providing them with everything they needed—food, housing, consumer goods, cars, education, and all that went with it— many boomers have never really wanted to grow up. In 1972 sociologist James S. Coleman had discerned the regressive character of the burgeoning new youth culture: "Locked into a world of their own creation, their own music and money and a license to do as they wished the young saw no reason to abandon this 'pleasing surrogate for maturity.'"[9]

Kenneth L. Woodward wrote in an article on "Young Beyond Their Years":

Adolescence is a period of intense self-absorption—a time for finding out who you are and the sort of person you can and ought to become. Adulthood, on the other hand, implies the development of character, competence and commitment, qualities essential for self-discipline, cooperation and taking care of others. By these standards, young Americans entering the 21st century are far less mature than their ancestors were at the beginning of the 20th. The difference is evident in all areas of youthful development: sex, love, marriage, education, and work.[10]

The result for young baby boomers is that many of them have not cut the apron strings from Mom and Dad. One of the surprising developments of the '80s was the number of baby boomers who went back home. It was not uncommon to find baby boomers who went to college and, after giving it a try in the work force, came back home to live with their parents when they did not make it. Another common situation was the divorced single mother returning home with children to live with her parents.

I know of one merged family consisting of two parents and ten baby boomer children. All of the children were out on their own. Wanting to move up in life, the parents contracted to build a beautiful four-bedroom house in which they thought they would spend the golden years of their retirement. But to their surprise, the children suddenly needed to move in with them. For two years they never had the partially completed house to themselves. One child had a drug problem and had to live with them. After they helped him through the problem and got him on his feet, another child went through a divorce and needed a place to stay. When she moved out, another daughter with her husband and two children moved in. They had sold their old house and misjudged the time it would take for the construction to be finished on their new one. So, when the husband had a heart attack, the older couple immediately made a decision. In one month, they sold the new house and bought a condo with one nice master bedroom and a small bedroom, which they set up as an office. In effect they made it impossible for the children to move home. They would no longer be available to bail out the kids when they got in trouble. As the mother said, "It just got to be too much. We need to be able to have our own lives. They have to make it on their own. We won't take care of them; they're adults, not children anymore."

This inability of some baby boomers to overcome their dependence on their parents is a reflection of a number of elements that affect the way baby boomers see themselves and live their lives. First, they are the product of the consumer culture that has taught them that their life is validated not by who they are but by what they have. Thousands of commercials have filled their minds with the message of consumerism: Meaning and purpose are found in what you wear, what you drive, where you live, and what you can afford.

The second element is living for the present. The first generation raised under the threat of nuclear annihilation, they learned to treat each moment as their last. There is little sense of history or future in the lives of boomers. In the business world the goal is short-term profits rather than long-range planning. In personal life, the goal is "going with the flow" and "living it up."

The third factor is instant gratification. Boomers want what they want *now*. The whole culture reflects this. In an age of huge government deficit spending and living on credit, commercials remind us during the Christmas season, "You don't have to pay till March." Fast-food, automatic tellers, one-minute management, and microwave dinners reflect the needs of a culture that hates to wait.

The fourth element is the trivialization of culture. Everything is marketable and sellable. When the Berlin Wall fell in late 1989, pieces of it were sold in stores during the Christmas season. Pepsi featured commercials showing the Berlin Wall and proclaiming "Peace on Earth" printed underneath the Pepsi logo. What was a moving historical event affecting the lives of millions of Europeans who were finding freedom was made into part of an ad campaign and sold in stores like pet rocks. In a culture that trivializes historical events, little value is placed on things that last. Whatever emotion is elicited by images that move the soul is denigrated by the association of the images with a product or with a need to buy the latest fad. The end result is rampant escapism, evident all across American culture. The slogan "escape to the movies" sums up what millions of Americans hope to do through a great variety of means. From the workaholic who wants to escape from the family, to the drug addict who seeks relief from the burdens of life, to the sports fan who lives and dies with a favorite team, to the Toys R Us kid who sings, "I don't want to grow up . . . ," to the hedonist who finds relief in the pleasures of the flesh, to the stargazer who revels in the scandals and troubles of a favorite celebrity, to the traditionalist who tries to go back to "the way it was," to the young-at-any-cost who exercises the body to skin and bones or alters the body through cosmetic surgery; boomers have found a slew of ways to flee the realities of life, to negate the changing panorama of the world, to insulate themselves from the ravages of time, to avoid dealing with their own mortality.

The focus on the now and the desire to escape have led people into the curious paradox of self-seeking. Thinking that one is free to choose one's own life, to be an authentic human being, to be free, one becomes dependent on others to define the self. Without a cultural history or family tradition afforded by the extended family of the past, the modern person is dependent on experts and advisors to lead the way. It is no accident that the '80s saw an explosion of a whole new genre, the self-help book. From raising children, to learning to love, to coping with husbands who cheat, to managing a business, to curing a baffling array of addictions, to becoming rich—a whole corps of self-helpers volunteered to steer boomers and their parents and children through the messy and complicated labyrinth of life.

In *The Culture of Narcissism*, Christopher Lasch writes:

Narcissism represents the psychological dimension of this dependence. Notwithstanding his occasional illusions of omnipotence, the narcissist depends on others to validate his self-esteem. He cannot live without an admiring audience. His apparent freedom from his family ties and institutional constraints does not free him to stand alone or to glory in his individuality. On the contrary, it contributes to his insecurity, which he can overcome only by seeing his "grandiose self" reflected in the attentions of others, or by attaching himself to those who radiate celebrity, power, and charisma. For the narcissist, the world is a mirror, whereas the rugged individualist saw it as an empty wilderness to be shaped to his own design.[11]

This endless looking in the mirror at one's own reflection carries with it a heavy burden—boredom. There is only so much navel gazing a person can do. How many tummy tucks and how much analysis can persons undergo before they realize that they are not so unique after all? Boomers are getting older and are facing the realization that they are not mythical gods free to do as they please for all eternity. But, in fact, they are mortal beings who face the reality of life and death.

This is not to say that everything about boomer self-seeking is wrong. In *The Denial of Death*, Ernest Becker notes that in humans "a working level of narcissism is inseparable from self-esteem, from a basic sense of self-worth."[12] Rather than a mere aberration, some degree of narcissism is key to the development of self-esteem. "It expresses the heart of the creature: the desire to stand out, to be the one in creation. When you combine natural narcissism with the basic need for self-esteem, you create a creature who has to feel himself an object of primary value: first in the universe, representing in himself all of life."[13]

But self-worth is not created in a vacuum; it does not happen spontaneously. It happens as a result of one's interactions with the world in which one finds meaning and purpose. Becker continues:

But man is not just a blind glob of idling protoplasm, but a creature with a name who lives in a world of symbols and dreams and not merely matter. His sense of self-worth is constituted symbolically, his cherished narcissism feeds on symbols, on an abstract idea of his own worth, an idea composed of sounds, words, and images, in the air, in the mind, on paper. And this means that man's natural yearning for organismic activity, the pleasures of incorporation and expansion, can be fed limitlessly in the domain of symbols and so into immortality. The single organism can expand into dimensions of worlds and times without moving a physical limb; it can take eternity into itself even as it gaspingly dies.[14]

Thus Steven Jobs, a baby boomer born in 1955, could start Apple Computer in his garage at the age of twenty and propel it into a multimillion dollar business on the strength of symbols and visionary ideas. Jobs' goal was to "change the world." Michael Murray, who was recruited out of Stamford University in 1980, remembers the messianic aura that surrounded Jobs as he unblushingly believed Apple Computer offered the dream of remaking the world through the personal computer.

> "This was the psychology of Mac. This was its passion," he says. "We believed fundamentally that we were changing the world. We honestly did. What Apple represented was the democratization of technology. Putting this enormously powerful thing called technology, which can be so scary, into the hands of the people."
>
> "Most of us were in our late twenties and early thirties," says Murray. "We missed the Beatles. We missed the civil rights movement. We missed Vietnam. Macintosh was our social revolution. We threw ourselves into it."[15]

In this way, the narcissism and self-seeking of baby boomers marks not only a peculiar problem, but also a special point of spiritual challenge, quest, and opportunity. For all of their narcissism, boomers seek what others have sought through other commitments and dreams—a place of meaning and purpose. They seek to be heroes in their own story, and in the world as they see it. Becker elaborates:

> It doesn't matter whether the cultural hero-system is frankly magical, religious, and primitive or secular, scientific, and civilized. It is still a mythical hero-system in which people serve in order to earn a feeling of primary value, of cosmic specialness, of ultimate usefulness to creation, of unshakable meaning. They earn this feeling by carving out a place in nature, by building an edifice that reflects human value: a temple, a cathedral, a totem pole, a skyscraper, a family that spans three generations. The hope and belief is that the things that man creates in society are of lasting worth and meaning, that they outlive or outshine death and decay, that man and his products count.[16]

There is no accounting for the influence of *The Wizard of Oz* on the psyche of the baby boomer generation. When I was a child, it was shown once a year on CBS, and I was allowed to stay up late to watch the whole thing. I remember watching it with my cousins and sisters and thought it was always shown on a holiday.

As a teenager I remember singing the songs with my friends at camp and doing the "Yellow Brick Road" dance, walking with our arms intertwined. When we were scared, we would say, "Lions and tigers and bears, oh my!" Even in college sometimes my fellow dormies and I would reenact some of the highlights of *The Wizard of Oz.* I never remember anyone doing the same thing with other childhood tales, such as Peter Pan or Cinderella.

Although the story of *The Wizard of Oz* seems to cherish the values of home and family, it is actually a story about a girl who has to make it on her own, who by accident becomes the heroine of the Munchkins. The most important scenes have to do with Dorothy's interaction with the Wizard of Oz, who she believes will solve all her problems and enable her to go home. But in the end, as Dorothy stands alone, abandoned by the Wonderful Wizard of Oz, she wonders if anyone can help her. It is only through the wisdom of the Good Witch that she is able to return from the colorized world of Oz to the black and white world of Kansas when she is told that she had to power to go home within herself.

The story of Dorothy in the Land of Oz is a powerful myth for the baby boom generation because it echoes so much of their experience of self-seeking. Madonna Kolbenschlag in *Lost in the Land Of Oz* says, "As an adult woman I found in Dorothy a mythic symbol that resonated with many of the turning points in my own growth to moral maturity—most of which would be described as acts of rebellion. No longer was she a childhood fantasy figure, but suddenly she took on a more heroic aspect. Especially in her encounters with the Wizard Dorothy seemed to portray so much of the reality of our experience of awakening and of seizing our own inner authority and autonomy as women."[17]

In the *Wizard of Oz* we see many predecessors to the movements that would affect baby boomers and their search for fulfillment and meaning. In Dorothy we find the assertive woman who finds herself; in the Tin Man, Scarecrow, and Lion, we find the bumbling men who find meaning by chasing after degrees and medals; in the Bad Witch and the Good Witch, we see an acceptance of a belief system outside of Christianity; in the rainbow we find the symbol of the New Age Movement; in the Emerald City we find the escapism that dominates much of our culture; and in the Wizard we find the failure of institutions to keep their promises.

One thing that makes Dorothy such an attractive heroine to boomers is the fact that she is an orphan, the abandoned one who has to find herself. There is within her journey a sense of not being a part of this world, of being just a visitor, not a complete participant. Her whole purpose is to return home, but even home is lacking a father and a mother. As much as she might love her aunt, there is no replacing the security and love of a parent. Perhaps more than anything else it is this feeling of lostness that captures the imagination of boomers. For it is only when we recognize our lostness in the modern-day world of Oz that we begin to find meaning in life. Madonna Kolbenschlag has captured the weight of this feeling.

> In spite of the illusion that partners, family, clan, nation, or church project in my life, my reality is that I am needy, love-starved, lonely, frightened of what may happen; I am bereft of models and mentors, detached from my history and roots, longing for connection. Only when I have accepted the reality of my orphan self, can I begin to really live.[18]

The net result of all of this is that boomers experience a great deal of ambivalence in their quest for meaning and purpose. Longing for home, family, and connection, they nevertheless feel compelled by brokenness, rootlessness, and loneliness to depend only upon themselves or the power of their efforts to find the end of the rainbow. Most of the time boomers put their efforts into trying to escape this deep sense of conflict. Most of the time the feelings are not even recognized. In quiet moments of reflection, most would admit to wanting to get away, if only for a moment, to find some kind of peace in a world that is running at warp speed.

The dilemma of the baby boomers is that they live in a culture that thrives on change, that is driven by trends, that eats up cultural identities and spits them out in a more palatable dish called "American." The reality is that America is built on rootlessness, loneliness, and brokenness. The person who is not willing to break with family, to move to a new city and face loneliness, and to pull up roots and try something new will have difficulty making it in a competitive world that thrives on innovation and change.

In *MexAmerica*, Lester D. Langley compares the cultural identity of the Euro-American baby boomer with the Hispanic who has roots in the Mexican culture.

> An American is a citizen of the United States. Without an ethnic or religious measure or, in the case of southerners, a sense of place, the American lacks a reassurance of cultural identity. We confront in the Hispanic—and especially in the Mexican—a people who do not define themselves with such self-denigrating slogans as "You Are What You Do" or consume, or as a truck advertisement declares, "You Are

What You Drive." No other society in the history of the world has searched so long for a meaningful cultural identity and failed in its quest. The lowliest Mexican fencejumper has a stronger sense of cultural identity than the American who employs him. He may not be able to read or write . . . but he knows who he is.[19]

What baby boomers are looking for they will never find in the American culture. By its very nature it brings them to a point of isolation. Until individuals of this generation face their lostness in this world, and admit that indeed they are orphans facing an uncertain future, they will continue to try to escape. For when a person truly finds self, that person finds an orphan self. Even Jesus on the cross modeled the lostness of the orphan when he said, "My God, my God, why have you forsaken me?" (Matt. 27:46). Strangely enough it is when one comes to this realization that one finds hope. In the acceptance of brokenness, loneliness, and rootlessness, a person is able to go beyond self-seeking to search for God.

2

THE SEARCH FOR GOD

Voice of Judas

Tell me what you think about your friends at the top
Who'd you think besides yourself's the pick of the crop?
Buddha was he where it's at? Is he where you are?
Could Mahomet move a mountain or was that just PR?
Did you mean to die like that? Was that a mistake or
Did you know your messy death would be a record-
*   breaker?*
Don't you get me wrong—I only want to know

CHOIR
Jesus Christ, Jesus Christ
Who are you? What have you sacrificed?
Jesus Christ Superstar
Do you think you're what they say you are?

"Superstar," Andrew Lloyd Webber and Tim Rice,
Jesus Christ Superstar, A Rock Opera, 1970.

Chapter Five

GODLINESS

It was unexpected. Like everything else the baby boomers embraced, it was unconventional, anti-institutional, emotional, experiential, and deeply personal. The chroniclers of the youth movement were caught off-guard, yet they reported it with the zeal they did with every other movement the boomers got caught up in. Their parents were at once touched and troubled, for even though it embraced some of their most cherished beliefs, it challenged their lifestyles at a level much deeper than the hippie movement ever could. The boomers turned on to Jesus.

I remember my experience with it. I was in eighth grade in May 1968. A lay witness team came to our church to witness to us about faith in Jesus Christ. I had never heard this message before, at least not presented in this way. They said, "Jesus was a personal savior who died on the cross to forgive you of your sins." They said things like, "I love you and God loves you" and "Even if you were the only person who ever lived on this earth, Jesus still would have given his life for you so you could be saved." This powerful message hit me at a time when I was most in need of love. I had done nothing exceptional in my life. I was a short teenager with red hair and freckles, glasses and braces, all the things that the Marlboro man was not. I was a good son, raised by loving parents, and had grown up in The Methodist Church but had not found anything that touched my heart.

I was a *Wonder Years'* kid, who watched the older members of my generation go off to war or to hippiedom while I was still trying to figure out how to get rubber bands to stay on my braces. But it was at just that moment of my greatest vulnerability and need that I heard the message that Jesus loved me. On a Sunday morning while the adults were in worship in the sanctuary, the youth were worshiping in the chapel. During our service the leader had an altar call, something which was completely foreign to my religious experience. While "How Great Thou Art" was being played on the organ, I went forward and accepted Jesus Christ. As I knelt on the floor, I said, "Dear Lord, I give my life to you to do as you will."

I will never forget that moment. Like a current of power, I felt the Spirit of God fill my heart. My friends also felt it, and as a group we raised ourselves from our knees and rushed into the main sanctuary and fell before the altar and prayed.

Of course the adults were shocked. The guest speaker was in the middle of his sermon, and here were twenty of their children weeping and crying right in the middle of the altar area. I do not know exactly what they did with us. Somehow the worship service was completed, and we finished the day with a farewell potluck for the lay mission group. But the aftermath of that experience sums up the problem many boomers faced with their passion for religious experience.

When we came back the next Sunday, the youth wanted to do something about the experience, but our parents were caught in a quandary. Our pastor, who had been gone the previous week, preached the same old sermon and was not comfortable with this kind of "religious emotionalism." Parents who had been made very uncomfortable by the passionate outburst of their children were trying to figure out how to handle this "experience." They hoped it was a fad or something that would pass with time.

Of course, on a deeper level, it challenged their beliefs in a God who was very logical, rational, upright, and socially acceptable. The biggest problem with the passionate response was that it looked like something only Holy Rollers would do, praying and singing and crying about their love for Jesus.

For years the mainline Protestant churches had done their best to separate themselves from the fundamentalists, the evangelicals, and especially the Pentecostal churches. Embracing the theology of neo-orthodoxy and preaching the Social Gospel, these churches hit their heyday in the mid-60s. In 1960 the Presbyterian Church with 4.2 million and the United Church of Christ with 2.2 million members reached their highest recorded membership. In 1965 the Methodist Church with 11 million, the Reformed Church in America with 3.9 million members, the Episcopal Church with 3.4 million, and the Disciples of Christ with 1.9 million, each recorded their highest membership in history. But by 1987 they had lost 25 percent of their combined membership, going from 22.9 million in 1965 to 17.6 million in 1987, a loss of over 5 million members.[1]

Their collective loss of members since 1965 is a reflection of their inability to keep and to attract the baby boom generation. For example, George Gallup Jr. and Jim Castelli report that "one in three Americans who were raised Methodist no longer identify with The United Methodist Church."[2]

It is ironic that the churches who were the most supportive of the civil rights movement, who were on the cutting edge of the feminist movement, who battled for inclusive language, and who were the most active in supporting human rights are now the churches that are hurting the most. Why is it that as boomers searched for God, they found the most powerful churches of the '50s and '60s to be meaningless? By answering this question we will go a long way in understanding the boomers' desire for godliness.

By all standards the '50s in America was a unique decade in the history of the nation. First, the United States economy dominated the world. From the perspective of the '90s, when America is challenged by a world economy and shares its leadership with Japan and Europe, it is hard to remember that in the '50s Japan and Europe were in ruins, devastated from the battles of World War II. It would take forty years for them to fully recover.

The only other power Americans had to fear was the Soviet Union, whose threat came in the form of the power to wage war and from their technological advances in space. But that country was always a poor competitor in the world of consumer goods and never threatened the American consumer market. As a result of this economic boom, American workers had extraordinary buying power. As Martha Farnsworth Riche says in *American Demographics*, "For the first and probably the only time in history, a man with less than average education could afford a house, two cars in the garage, three or four kids, and a nonworking wife."[3]

Second, the education gap between men and women was the second largest gap recorded in the century. The percentage of women who were college graduates was 22 percent in 1910, 34 percent in 1920, 39 percent in 1930, and 41 percent in 1940. But in 1950 there was a huge drop to 23 percent, the lowest since 1910. In 1960 it went to 35 percent, to 41 percent in 1970, 47 percent in 1980, to a majority in 1987 of 51 percent.[4]

Claudia Wallis reported in a *Time* cover story called "Onward, Women" that in the '90s 54 percent of undergraduates will be women while in the '50s two-thirds of female undergraduates did not even graduate.[5] This drop in educational attainment by women was a sign of a pattern that typified the American culture of the '50s. Rather than building on the historical gains of the feminist movement, which culminated in women's gaining the right to vote in 1920, and progressing from the experience of working in all areas of the economy during World War II, the chief goal of women in the '50s was to have a husband and a family. The words of a college girl, which are found in Betty

Friedan's *The Feminine Mystique*, give us a hint of the attitudes of the
time toward women's education.

> Maybe we should take it more seriously. But nobody wants to gradu-
> ate and get into something where they can't use it. If your husband is
> going to be an organization man, you can't be too educated. The wife
> is awfully important for the husband's career. You can't be too
> interested in art, or something like that.

Here words convey some startling assumptions that made up the
belief system of her generation. A woman should not be too educated.
Why? Because she does not want to appear to be smarter than her man.
If a wife is important for the husband's career, the reverse was also true,
for in the mindset of the '50s, a woman could find value and meaning
only by being a good wife and mother. Betty Friedan said:

> In the fifteen years after World War II, this mystique of feminine
> fulfillment became the cherished and self-perpetuating core of con-
> temporary American culture. Millions of women lived their lives in
> the image of those pretty pictures of the American suburban house-
> wife, kissing their husbands goodbye in front of the picture window,
> depositing their stationwagonful of children at school, and smiling
> as they ran the new electric waxer over the spotless kitchen floor. . . .
> Their only dream was to be perfect wives and mothers; their high-
> est ambition to have five children and a beautiful house, their only
> fight to get and keep their husbands. They had no thought for
> the unfeminine problems of the world outside the home; they
> wanted the men to make the major decisions. They gloried in their
> role as women, and wrote proudly on the census blank: "Occupa-
> tion: housewife." [6]

It was this belief that a woman could only be fulfilled by having a
family that fueled the baby boom. The birthrate climbed to 27 per
thousand in the mid-50s. From 1945 to 1946 there was a jump in births
in America from 2,873,000 to 3,426,000. Each successive year added
more births until 1954 when the total went to 4,102,000 and stayed
over 4,000,000 each year until 1964. [7] In 1957 when births hit an all-
time record high of 4.3 million, proud census officials pointed out that
in 1957 one baby was born every seven seconds.

What made this unusual was that in most other Western countries,
after a brief baby boom following the war, the birthrate dropped. Only
Canada, Australia, and New Zealand kept up with the high rate of the
U.S. So high was this birthrate that it rivaled and sometimes surpassed

the birthrate of underdeveloped countries, where the much-talked-about population explosion was taking place.[8]

Adding to the baby boom was the huge number of teenage marriages. In 1953 almost a third of American females had married by the time they reached 19. The median age at first marriage dropped from 25.9 for males and 21.9 for females in 1900 to an all-time low of 22.8 for males and 20.3 for females in the mid-50s.[9] In 1900, 48 percent of women aged 20-24 were married. By 1960 71 percent of women aged 20-24 were married, which compares to 37.5 percent in 1989.[10]

My oldest sister was engaged at sixteen and married when she was nineteen, during the heyday of this marriage mania. She has always had a hard time explaining to her daughter how this came to be. Today's nineteen-year-old woman has barely started college or a career, and most would not want to think of settling down with a husband and a family until they were at least twenty-two, if not older. Before marriage they want to establish their own identity; their education and career come first.

More tellingly, a 1990 Yankelovich Clancy Shulman poll commissioned by *Time* of young people aged 18 to 24 shows that 85 percent of them think it is more likely that their marriages will end in a divorce when compared to their parents' generation. At the same time, if given the opportunity, 66 percent of young women said they would be interested in staying at home and raising their children.[11]

While today's young women take a cold-edged look at their futures, the women of the '50s were caught up in what Betty Friedan labeled "the feminine mystique." A number of cultural trends produced this mindset. Of primary importance was the effect of World War II. When talking about love and family, the war years from 1941 to 1945 were the lonely years. Millions of young men in their prime became part of the huge effort to defeat Germany and Japan. As the men went off to war, the women were left behind. Those who had husbands or lovers wondered if they would ever come back. Those who did not have a love wondered if there would be one for them when the war was over. Friedan states, "When the men came back there was a headlong rush into marriage. The lonely years when husbands or husbands-to-be were away at war—or could be sent away at a bomb's fall—made women particularly vulnerable to the feminine mystique."[12]

Another factor was the widespread acceptance of Freudian views on the nature and function of males and females based on the idea that anatomy is destiny. One of the most influential books of the time was *Modern Woman: The Lost Sex* written by Marynia Farnham and Ferdinand Lundberg. Published in 1947 the book postulated that there were intrinsic differences between men and women that predispose them toward natural tendencies in life. Men are naturally strong, aggressive, independent, rational, and competitive, so they are the workers, the protectors, and leaders of society. On the other hand, women are naturally soft, passive, emotional, obedient, gentle, and maternal, so they are the natural mothers, wives, and homemakers. Society functions best if each sex follows its own role in life. "If individuals try to deny their natural instincts and perform functions relegated to the opposite sex, they will become unhappy, perhaps even neurotic, their marriages will suffer, and society will suffer. The normal woman can reach full contentment and happiness only by being a passive, dependent mother and wife."[13]

In light of the gains women have made in education, business, and careers, this sounds outrageous. Although family is important, to say that women can find meaning in life only by being passive mothers and wives is to deny the ability of women to contribute to society in many different ways. Now that women are doctors, lawyers, pastors, governors, engineers, plumbers, and members of the police force, everyone benefits from the resources and insights they bring to their professions. Claudia Wallis reported that since 1960 the number of women in the work force has grown from 34.8 percent to 57.8 percent. In the legal profession alone the number of women lawyers and judges has increased from 7,500 to 180,000.[14]

But in the 1950s the view that a woman's natural role was in the home was expressed by educated Americans and taught in high schools and universities as scientific fact. While men were to be taught in the sciences and mathematics, women were best suited for courses in home economics, ceramics, and flower arranging, which prepared them for their role as the happy homemaker. While women's enrollment in college almost doubled during the '50s, only a third graduated. More than half the female students who dropped out did so because, as people joked, they had gained their MRS degree and were now working on their Ph.T, "Putting Hubby Through."[15]

Adding to this was the persuasive message of the mass media, which was a prime purveyor of these-well defined roles for men and women. On television Lucy was the zany housewife who always got herself into impossible situations. Harriet Nelson was the perfect wife and mother who stayed at home. Alice Kramden was the battling wife who was always caught up in one household chore or another.

In the movies of the '50s women played three types of roles: the girl next door (Doris Day), the sexy bombshell (Marilyn Monroe), and the temptress (Elizabeth Taylor). These roles were quite different from the ones played by actresses such as Bette Davis, Katherine Hepburn, and Greta Garbo, who played career women with complex identities in the movies of the '30s and '40s. In contrast, the '50s woman was defined by the one-dimensional characters played by actresses such as Marilyn Monroe, who was seen as the epitome of womanhood in all her breathless sexiness, the proverbial blonde without a brain.

Women's magazines, which were a powerful force in the '50s, pushed this stereotypical image with articles such as, "How to Snare a Male," "Should I Stop Work When We Marry?," "Are You Training Your Daughter to Be a Wife?," "Really a Man's World, Politics," "Femininity Begins at Home," "Have Babies When You're Young," and "The Business of Running a Home." Friedan says of these images:

> These new happy housewife heroines seem strangely younger than the spirited career girls of the thirties and forties. They seem to get younger all the time—in looks, and a childlike kind of dependence. They have no vision of the future, except to have a baby. The only active growing figure in their world is the child. The housewife heroines are forever young, because their own image ends in childbirth. . . . They must keep having babies, because the feminine mystique says there is no other way for a woman to be a heroine.
>
> It is my thesis that the core of the problem for women today is not sexual but a problem of identity—a stunting or evasion of growth that is perpetuated by the feminine mystique. It is my thesis that as the Victorian culture did not permit women to accept or gratify their basic sexual needs, our culture does not permit women to accept or gratify their basic need to grow and fulfill their potentialities as human beings, a need which is not solely defined by their sexual role.[16]

This need to stay within proscribed roles leads us to the third unique characteristic of the '50s, which was the need for conformity. As the economy prospered and as men returned from the war, there was a mass migration from the country to the city. As men expanded their horizons, they moved to where industries provided jobs, and they moved from the farm to the suburb. Although boomers may long for the traditional family life of the '50s, the parents of boomers experienced the '50s as a great time of transition. People who had been raised on farms or in small towns found themselves in teeming neighborhoods of families. In Los Angeles the first freeway was built, and for the first time men "commuted" to work, which is something as natural to us as having a computer in the office.

Separated from their extended families, which had supported them in the past, the pioneers of the '50s joined clubs, played bridge, volunteered in community organizations, and went to church. Unlike the baby boom generation, boomer parents were joiners who wanted to belong, who needed to find a sense of community.

It was in this setting of a growing economy, well-defined roles for men and women, and the need to belong that the mainline churches boomed in the '50s. During the late '50s Methodists started one new congregation every three days and Baptists started one every five days. In 1957 the U.S. Census reported that 96 percent of Americans cited a specific religious affiliation when asked, "What is your religion?" In the atmosphere of the cold war and McCarthyism, it was considered patriotic to be a Protestant, Catholic, or Jew, as opposed to the anti-God, atheistic Communists. In 1954 President Dwight D. Eisenhower said, "Our government makes no sense unless it is founded on a deeply felt religious faith—and I don't care what it is."[17]

This attitude expressed by the president, of not caring what the religious faith of people was as long as they had it, was one of the chief characteristics of '50s style religion. Rather than stressing the need for a particular brand of faith, religion was expressed as a trans-denominational message, which stressed peace of mind and confident living. Rather than probing the social ills of society and fighting racism, materialism, and sexism, this "faith in faith" mentality was carefully mixed with Freudian insights and depth psychology to offer peace and harmony to people who were trying to live in the "age of anxiety."

Best-selling books of the time included *Peace of Mind* by Reformed Rabbi Joshua Loth Liebman, *A Man Called Peter* by Catherine Marshall, and *Peace of Soul* by Monsignor Fulton J. Sheen, who became the first TV religious personality. The leader of the pack was Norman Vincent Peale, a former Methodist turned Congregationalist, whose book, *The Power of Positive Thinking*, was published in 1952, stayed on top of the best-seller list for 112 consecutive weeks, and sold more copies than any other book except the Bible in 1954.[18] In the preface of his book, Peale gives a summation of his philosophy:

> The powerful principles contained herein are not my invention but are given to us by the greatest Teacher who ever lived and who still lives. This book teaches applied Christianity; a simple yet scientific system of practical techniques of successful living that works.[19]

Peale's approach was not much different from that of Lafayette Ronald Hubbard, who published a best-seller in 1950 called *Dianetics: The Modern Science of Mental Health*. This book espoused the beliefs of Scientology, which Hubbard started in 1940. It combined psychology with scientific analysis to help a "preclear," one who is discovering things about her or himself and who is becoming clear, to become clear through sessions with a trained auditor who used an "E" meter to cure all psychoses, neuroses, psychosomatic illnesses, coronary diseases, arthritis, and other ailments. Based on the theory of the brain as a perfect calculating machine, Hubbard's work would become a publishing sensation, which is still touted in magazine ads and on television and radio as the best-selling self-help book ever published.[20]

Another author, Anne Morrow Lindbergh, topped them all in 1955 with her *Gift from the Sea*, a book addressed to housewives who were distraught with the emptiness of their lives. Ignoring specific institutional appeals, she drew on the long American tradition of mysticism to calm the fears of her readers.[21]

In conflict with this generalized approach to religion was the upsurge of revivalism as personified in Billy Graham, which proclaimed the old-time religion based on personal experience and commitment to Christ, a strict code of morality, gospel hymns, and simple preaching. After a tent-meeting revival in Los Angeles in 1949, Graham vaulted into national prominence with his Billy Graham Evangelistic Association, which used all available mass media to promote his evangelical brand of Christianity. Traveling from city to city, Graham held huge outdoor rallies in stadiums across the country, calling on people to make a personal commitment to Jesus Christ.

Unlike the revivalists of the past such as Dwight L. Moody and Billy Sunday, Billy Graham's constituencies did not come from the old mainline congregations. Instead, his chief support came from conservatives within the larger Protestant denominations or from churches opposed to the ecumenical movement. As successful as he was, Graham's method did not make a significant number of those who made decisions into good churchgoers. Many persons who went forward at an altar call in a stadium never made it to worship on Sunday at the local church.

While Norman Vincent Peale was promoting his "success through Christianity" message and Billy Graham was preaching repentance and belief in a personal savior, mainline churches were caught up in something called "Parish Renewal." Seeking to halt the inroads of patriotic piety and success-oriented religion, mainline pastors embraced the liturgical movement and neoorthodoxy. While by outward appearances mainline denominations were recording record years in membership, worship attendance, sales of religious books, and new church construction, inwardly there were great concerns to be faced.

Leonard I. Sweet wrote about the '50s in an article called "The Modernization of Protestant Religion in America":

> Religious and biblical literacy had seldom been lower. Denominational identities were eroded by the forces of public religion, bureaucratization, and modernism's devaluation of tradition. Allegiances were becoming less to denominations than to movements and causes within denominations. The fifties were the triumphant decade for the definition of church membership as going to church rather than being the church, with the individualistic notion of the church as one's private chapel so rampant that gambits had to be devised to thaw the cold wars going on inside the sanctuaries themselves—guest registration pads passed down the pews, "rituals of friendship" during worship, and their more stylish updating in the 1960s as "the kiss of peace."[22]

Ordained ministers in mainline churches were more likely to be seen as counselors than prophets and caretakers than visionaries. The rigid standards of education required of the ordained minister brought ministerial students into a bewildering array of biblical criticism. These studies aimed to strip away the "myths of the Bible" in order to find the "historical Jesus," thus exposing students to the minimalist theology of neo-orthodoxy, which denied to history or to the world any capacity for divine revelation except when the kerygmatic "moment of faith" took place. Thus ordained ministers were urged by Karl Barth to stand in the pulpit with the Bible in one hand and the daily paper in the other. Sweet says:

> Theologians specialized in hermeneutical and methodological crossword puzzles, whose answers were absorbing to the players but useless to the wider public. . . . After having created a theological rain forest impenetrable to the unguided mind, both theologians and the clergy they trained only reluctantly served as guides to lay persons brave enough to wish to enter.[23]

Along with complex theologies came the liturgical movement, which in the '60s and '70s sought to bring the laity into an experience of worship whose origins could be traced to the romantic religious revival of the nineteenth century in Great Britain and on the continent among both Roman Catholics and Protestants. A high church form of worship was established as the norm, with congregations reading liturgies and pastors leading worship in the style of priests.

Rather than bringing the laity into a closer experience of worship, the theology of neo-orthodoxy and the high church style of worship separated clergy even further from their congregations. Instead of giving in to "popular" tastes, pastors saw themselves as the harbingers of culture and spirituality to the uneducated masses.

Ironically, while the Catholics headed toward Vatican II with the intent of opening up worship to the laity with the use of vernacular languages, and while the public embraced the simple message of the half-hour sitcom, mainline churches sanctioned a style of worship that relegated the laity into penitent observers of ritual and practice. Of the era of the '50s, church historian Sydney E. Ahlstrom says that the church "failed to meet religious needs." With a large influx of a mobile people who found a social identification in the church, the church "muffed its chance" to change lives.

> Put more analytically, the so-called revival led to a sacrifice of theological substance, which in the face of the harsh new realities of the 1960s left both clergy and laity demoralized and confused. . . . Americans began to sense the dawn of a new age in their spiritual history, a time of reorientation and beginning again, in which the past experience and present situation of every tradition would be opened for reexamination.[24]

The first salvo of this reexamination came in 1957 when the National Guard of Arkansas stood off the assault by whites on a few black children in the segregated Central High School of Little Rock. No longer could churches keep the question of racial justice in a closet. It was hard to look past the fact that in America the worship hour on Sunday mornings was the most segregated hour of the week.

With the National Council of Churches playing a leading role, mainline preachers took on the mantle of the prophet of God who condemned the racist practices of society and the church. While the shining moments were in the civil rights marches led by Martin Luther King, Jr., mainline church pastors pushed the Social Gospel to its limits while forgetting the pastoral and spiritual needs of the congregation. It was not unusual to find the pastor-prophet at war with the congregation who grew tired of the pastor's condemnation of their materialistic lifestyles and racist attitudes, while in the name of justice he/she asked for greater benefits and a higher salary.

Even more nerve-racking to the regular church member was the propensity of denominational leaders to take up the banner of all kinds of causes and issues that the church member opposed. In a more subtle brand of elitism, these leaders followed a fashionable leftward bias that looked down on patriotism and manifested itself in empowerment money for causes such as Angela Davis's defense fund ($10,000 from the United Presbyterian Church in the U.S.A. in 1970), for the "Alianza of New Mexico," and James Forman's "Black Manifesto Movement" ($40,000 and $200,000, respectively, from the Episcopal Church in 1969), and the finishing touch, $85,000 from the World Council of Churches in 1978 to the Patriotic Front in Zimbabwe. A *National Review* cartoon showed this bewildering use of church monies by picturing Vietcong General Giap receiving a telegram that read, "The Episcopal Diocese of New York stands shoulder to shoulder with you in your resistance to American aggression."[25]

Tom Wolfe, the penetrating social commentator and journalist, put it quite bluntly in a passage from "The Me Decade and the Third Great Awakening."

> The key—one and all decided—was to "modernize" and "update" Christianity. So the Catholics gave the nuns outfits that made them look like World War II Wacs. The Protestants set up "beatnik coffee houses" in the church basement for poetry reading and bongo playing. . . . Both the priests and the preachers carried placards in civil rights marches, gay rights marches, women's rights marches, prisoners' rights marches, bondage lovers' rights marches, or any other marches, so long as they might appear hip to the urban young people.
>
> In fact, all the strenuous gestures merely made the church look like rather awkward and senile groupies of secular movements. The much-sought-after Urban Young People found the Hip Churchmen to be an embarrassment, if they noticed them at all. What finally started attracting young people to Christianity was something the churches had absolutely nothing to do with: namely the psychedelic or hippie movement. . . .
>
> Today it is precisely the most rational, intellectual, secularized, modernized, updated, relevant religions—all the brave, forward-looking Ethical Culture, Unitarian, and Swedenborgian movements of only yesterday—that are finished, gasping, breathing their last. What the Urban Young People want from religion is a little . . . *Hallelujah!* . . . and *talking in tongues!* . . . *Praise God!*[26]

Thus it was quite a shock to find baby boomers turning on to Jesus in the late '60s and early '70s. Baby boomers who had left the institutionalized church in droves now found themselves embroiled in an unexpected movement, the Jesus Movement.

In June 1971 the cover of *Time* proclaimed "The Jesus Revolution." In February of the same year *Look* gave extensive coverage to the movement in an article entitled, "The Jesus Movement Is Upon Us." It proclaimed that a crusade, a fundamentalist, Christ-as-personal-Savior revival had caught on in California and showed signs that it would sweep East and take the nation by storm. It said the new evangelists were the young, spreading an old-time, Bible-toting, witness-giving kind of faith. With great joy they told people to turn on to Jesus, as he was coming—soon.[27]

Calvary Chapel of Costa Mesa, California, was at the forefront of the Jesus Revolution. In a two-year period in the mid-'70s, Calvary Chapel performed over 8,000 baptisms in the Pacific Ocean and was instrumental in bringing over 20,000 conversions to the Christian faith. When Chuck Smith became pastor of Calvary Chapel in the late '60s, he saw a flood of hippies and flower children on the beach and was moved to minister to them. The church, which only had twenty-six members, began to grumble when some of the poorly garbed youth started coming to the church. Early in his ministry at Calvary Chapel, Smith told his leaders:

> I don't want it ever said that we preach an easy kind of Christian experience at Calvary Chapel. But I also do not want to make the same mistake that the Holiness Church made thirty years ago. Without knowing it, they drove out and lost a whole generation of young people with a negative no-movie, no-dance, no-smoke gospel. Let us at Calvary not be guilty of this same mistake. Instead, let us trust God and emphasize the work of the Holy Spirit within individual lives. It is exciting and much more real and natural to allow the Spirit to dictate change. Let us never be guilty of forcing our Western Christian subculture of clean-shaven, short-hair styles or dress on anyone. We want change to come from the inside out. We simply declare that drugs, striving to become a millionaire, or making sports your whole life is not where true fulfillment or ultimate meaning lies. Because the end of all these goals is emptiness and disappointment.[28]

It was pastors such as Chuck Smith who were able to reach baby boomers with a message of acceptance and love that caused many to find faith in Jesus Christ. Tal Brooke, a baby boomer who had been turned off by "a small-minded judgmentalism" which was often accompanied by a "chilly aloofness" in the churches he attended, turned to Eastern religions because "the love that is so enthrallingly reported in the New Testament church wasn't very evident in those modern churches."

After a long search for God, which took him as far away as India, he found God one Sunday when he walked into Calvary Chapel. Of that day he says, "I felt an abundant flow of love the moment I walked through the door. There was not even a fleeting hint of judgmentalism here. Rather, I felt a terrific sense of belonging."[29]

The Jesus Movement personified what boomers had been looking for all along, a personal experience of godliness that said, "I am important," "I count," "Jesus loves me." Not finding this message in mainline American religion, they started their own nondenominational churches or lived in Christian communes or infiltrated established churches in the hope of saving their parents' generation.

Perhaps the most important religious event of the early '70s was the opening of the controversial rock opera, *Jesus Christ Superstar* on Broadway in 1971. It was the first Broadway musical ever to have grown from an LP album that sold in the millions before its opening. Written by Andrew Lloyd Webber, age 23, and Tim Rice, age 26, the opera was a nonstop, pulsating, rock 'n' roll experience that asked the questions baby boomers were asking about faith and God and Jesus. At the time, *Christianity Today* said, "Many Christians have ignored this generation's questions about Jesus. For those who will listen, *Superstar* tells what young people are saying."[30]

Two characters generated the most controversy. Mary Magdalene sang, "I Don't Know How to Love Him," which insinuated a love relationship that made conservatives uncomfortable. Judas sang "Superstar," asking Jesus why he had let things get so out of hand, which challenged the belief in a divinely inspired Jesus who had it all together. Rice said one of the intents of the musical was "to show the way people react to him." Jesus himself was portrayed as a humanitarian thinker and the charismatic leader of a dissident movement who became a victim of his fame and power and died as a martyr for his people.

What made *Superstar* important was that it made Jesus accessible to the baby boomer generation. Its message was packaged in a way that boomers could relate to, and it gave them a chance to examine their beliefs in relationship to this Jesus. It scratched the core of what many boomers had been seeking, a religious experience that dug beneath the ritual and rationality of their parents' religion and challenged the technological materialism that dominated so much of their lives. Beyond the protests, the long hair, the hippie clothing, the adolescent rebellion, and the loud music was a secret desire to be godly, to be made whole, to be one with the creation, to find meaning and purpose, to belong.

Not finding what they needed in institutionalized religion, millions of boomers went on a search that would lead them away from Jesus and the church that proclaimed him. Many went on a journey into dark and strange places and have never come back.

Chapter Six

SUPERNATURALISM

In the world of the supernatural, everything is possible and nothing is unbelievable. It is a world populated by angels and devils, extraterrestrials and mystics, spirit guides and Buddhas, ancient voices and channelers. Its source of knowledge ranges from the gnostic gospels to *Siddhartha*, from Native American religions to Eastern mysticism, from astrology to the channeled teachings of the ascended masters. Its tools include Ouija boards, tarot cards, runes, crystals, I Ching, the *Tibetan Book of the Dead*, star charts, numerology, hypnosis, and the Bible. Its dialogue is filled with words like karma, the light, at-one-ment, the wave, channeling, ESP, reincarnation, cosmic energy, inner healing, holistic health, psychic ability, chakras, and the New Age.

To enter into this strange new world, you need only to be open and willing to seek the god that is within, to find the divine self, to realize that you are "God." Its basic worldview is ignored by mainline Protestants, railed at by conservative fundamentalists, and strangely enough, embraced in some ways by Pentecostals and charismatics. Like the black market in a totalitarian country, supernaturalism makes up the vast underbelly of the American religious economy. It is a world that has become especially appealing to the baby boom generation.

The musical *Hair*, which in 1969 scandalized theatergoers because of its nude dancing, enthralled boomers with its message of peace, love, and acceptance, which was a sign of the Age of Aquarius. The song from the musical made famous by the Fifth Dimension, "Let the Sunshine In"* became a number-one hit with its words proclaiming the "dawning" of the Age of Aquarius.

Catch words and phrases such as "harmony," "golden living dreams of visions," "mystic crystal revelations," and "love will steer the stars" captured the imagination and placed this Aquarian vision in opposition to the scientific worldview, which had given us two world wars, Vietnam, and the bomb. The musical was filled with dancing, energy, freedom, and joy. It promoted a new vision of the world where the color of one's skin did not divide and where love and peace ruled.

In many ways the musical was the personification of the highest ideals of the counterculture, which pulled its ideas from sources outside of mainstream America and was just as comfortable talking about realigning a person's chakras as another person would be talking about the latest baseball scores. The worldview of the counterculture embraced nature and valued the stuff of this earth over the urban world of concrete and glass. It was a reaction to the overvaluing of technology as the panacea for all the world's problems.

Theodore Roszak, in *The Making of a Counter Culture*, points out the flaws in the scientific worldview and says that in a scientific culture "objectivity as a state of being fills the very air we breathe." The scientific mentality gripping us in all we say, feel, and do, "becomes the very soul of society."[1] In a very real sense objectivity is the myth of our age.

The problem with this objective consciousness is that the only one who can have it is the dispassionate scientist whose goal is to be devoid of all emotions, feelings, and opinions in order to make an objective analysis of whatever he or she is studying. As a result, all of life is viewed as a grand experiment that can be measured, collated, analyzed, evaluated, surveyed, and classified.

The world is divided between the "scientist," whose chief characteristic is a hard core of rationality, and the "subjects" of scientific inquiry who have messy emotions, feelings, and, worst of all, opinions, which tend to skew the findings of the so-called experts. At the extreme, the objective, rational scientist can talk dispassionately of winning a nuclear war in which our losses will only be a few million people while the enemy will lose almost their total population.

In the name of scientific inquiry, soldiers were exposed to nuclear blasts to test their readiness to fight in such conditions; students were given LSD to study their reactions to this new wonder drug; healthy animals were subjected to surgeries and injections to test new methods; artificial hearts were placed into the chests of dying patients; brain cells of fetuses were scooped out and used to try to cure the diseases of elderly patients; prisoners were given any number of pharmaceutical products to see their results; and drug companies tried out new drugs in third world countries to perfect them for the North American market.

The perfect manifestation of this objective consciousness is the creation of the machine that can process millions of bits of information in a second and can measure, tabulate, and perform skills in endless repetition with flawless objectivity. When something goes wrong, it can be fixed simply, without fuss, and you do not have to pay its social security. To make this great machine work you have to regulate time into a rigid rhythm of the clock, which keeps all things tied together in perfectly measurable, controllable segments of existence. Any other experience of time is mystical or supernatural.

The biggest problem with the scientific myth is that it robs life of the experience of joy. Since everything can be measured in relationship to some kind of objective scale hatched from the brain of the objective scientist, nothing in this world is special, wondrous, or extraordinary. Even life itself has come about because of an accidental thrashing of atoms in the atmosphere. Roszak comments:

> Consider the strange compulsion our biologists have to synthesize life in a test tube—and the seriousness with which this project is taken. Every dumb beast of the earth knows without thinking once about it how to create life: it does so by seeking delight where it shines most brightly. But, the biologist argues, once we have done it in a laboratory, then we shall really know what it is all about. Then we shall be able to improve upon it![2]

With the supremacy of the rational, objective, scientific worldview comes the death of joy and experience. Objectivity breeds mutated personalities that can see nature only as something to be conquered, view people as things to be persuaded and surveyed, and think God is dead. In contrast to the myth of objectivity, supernaturalism says there is a vast realm of experience that embraces all that life has to offer, that places one's heart at the disposal of the creative forces of the universe, that focuses on the making rather than on the made, and that enables a person to become a whole being filled with the totality of all the experiences and emotions that make a person human.

In the late '60s and early '70s technocracy's children shed the myth of objectivity like a snake's skin and embraced experience in all its manifestations in the world of the supernatural. They turned to the East and grappled with Buddhism. They resonated with its idea of faith as not an ideological underpinning, but rather as a mystic vision. Buddhism represented a tradition that taught that you had to close your eyes to objective reality in order to perceive the wholeness and beauty of all that is. This had great appeal to a generation that felt itself drowning in a sea of words without emotional roots and personal connections.

Buddhism also gained adherents because of its teaching to become one with nature. This is in sharp contrast with traditional Western Christianity, which seemed to teach that humanity is nature's overlord. In the nineteenth and twentieth centuries Christians have exercised this lordship in a way that has brought ecological ruin to the world. Buddhism, on the other hand, says that we are not separate from the world, but are part of it, that to find oneself one has to be in union with all of creation.

Another core teaching of Buddhism that is in contrast to Christianity is that its scnsc of salvation is ncgativc in dircction. Buddhism does not aim at building the kingdom of God or moving on to perfection or maturing in Christ or redeeming a fallen world. Instead, for the Buddhist the world is unreal and must be "let go" in order for a believer to find oneness with the universe.[3]

Psychiatrist David Elkind in 1971 commented on youth's desire to break free from the rationalistic conceit of the West. He commented that the youth of the '70s were turned off by the dead symbols of institutional religion but still wished to explore spiritual matters. This search for meaningful symbols of spirituality led them to Eastern religions because they seemed to be so mysterious. This was in contrast to Western society whose deification of reason had intellectualized religion to the point of alienating persons from their feelings and inner world.[4]

Beyond Buddhism other baby boomers in the late '60s and early '70s discovered religious meaning in homegrown movements such as Synanon, Aria, and Scientology, which began to take on a spiritual atmosphere. Esalen Institute, a lodge perched on a cliff overlooking the Pacific Ocean in Big Sur, California, specialized in group encounter sessions, which were aimed at getting people to bare their souls and strip away their defensive façades. Psychedelic communes and new left communes took up the same method to help one another find the real "Me."

Tom Wolfe says, "And what will the Real Me be like? It is at this point that the new movements tend to take on a religous or spiritual atmosphere. At one point or another they arrive at an axiom first propounded by the Gnostic Christians some eighteen hundred years ago: namely, that at the apex of every human soul there exists a spark of the light of God. . . . He who has dug himself out from under the junk heap of civilization can discover it."[5]

Other boomers sought to manipulate nature and time by use of occult practices. In the singles scene, the first question asked by a prospective suitor was, "What's your sign?" rather than "What's your name?" Astrology became the in thing with young and old alike. Twenty-five years later even the president of the United States would be rearranging his schedule according to his horoscope. The wide appeal of astrology was soon followed by other occult practices such as tarot cards, numerology, Ouija boards, witchcraft, and satanism.

Capitalizing on this interest was the film, *The Exorcist*, which in 1973 became the top money-maker of its time. I remember going to the movie with a group of friends from college. We stood in a line for three hours to get in. When we finally made it into the theater, we ended up in the front row.

Of course the movie scared us to death, not because of its special effects or gory scenes, but because the story line was so believable. None of us had any problem believing that a girl could be possessed by the devil and that, in the end, the church would be ineffective in dealing with it. After all, it echoed the experience many of us had had with the occult.

After I became a Christian, I went through a number of experiences not unknown to members of the baby boom generation. Wanting the same powerful experience of the Holy Spirit I had felt when I became a Christian and not finding it again in my church, my friends and I went in a different direction; we discovered the Ouija board. In ninth and tenth grade the Ouija board became my faithful companion. I took it with me on church campouts and introduced its power to my friends. We went through elaborate ceremonies of our own devising, lighting particular candles and making sure the shadow of the cross was on the board at all times to protect us from evil spirits.

At one church campout while our parents were in the main cabin, a group of us were using the board. It said that one of the girls had an evil spirit in her. In order to get rid of it, I was to do a series of incantations to take the evil spirit from her and put it into me to save her soul. Without thinking, I followed its instructions to the letter and that night I opened myself up to the influence of an evil spirit. Soon I began having strange and violent dreams, some of which came true.

As I went through high school, I had something of a double life—the Christian who went to church and the occultist who used all sorts of paraphernalia to try to foretell the future. All through this my church was naively ignorant or reasonably tolerant of the whole thing. No one ever said anything was wrong with it. After all, it was just a game, wasn't it?

During my first year in college a friend took me to his black Pentecostal congregation where I was confronted with the enormity of what I was doing. That night, during an altar call, I went through a spiritual battle which freed me from the evil power that had been oppressing me. Later I was told that through prayer and faith in Jesus, I needed to close the doors on my occult practices, and I was freed from the hold the occult had on me during my youth.

No words are adequate to explain how all this happened; no concepts wrap it up in a neat theological package. All I can say is that I know it happened to me. It is part of my spiritual journey and as a result I have no doubt about the power of God or the reality of a supernatural world beyond our understanding and easy definitions. Other boomers had similar experiences coming out from under the power of drugs, especially LSD. With these experiences in mind, the great search for God and spiritual truth led boomers in many different directions in their youth.

Tom Wolfe called it the "third great awakening," which was distinctive in that it was not tied to one particular faith or one denomination, but was tied to the one great concern that everyone could get excited about, the concern for "Me." In talking about the religious movements of the early '70s, he said:

> "Let's talk about Me." They begin with the most delicious look inward; with considerable narcissism, in short. When the believers bind together into religions, it is always with the sense of splitting off from the rest of society. We, the enlightened (lit by the sparks at the apexes of our souls), hereby separate ourselves from the lost souls around us. Like all religions before them, they proselytize—but always promising the opposite of nationalism; a City of Light that is above it all. There is no ecumenical spirit within this Third Great Awakening. If anything, there is a spirit of schism. The contempt the various gurus and seers have for one another is breathtaking. One has only to ask, say, Oscar Ichazo of Arica about Carlos Castaneda or Werner Erhard of est to learn that Castaneda is a fake and Erhard is a shallow sloganeer. It's exhilarating!—to watch the faithful split off from one another to seek ever more perfect and refined crucibles in which to fan the Divine spark . . . and to *talk about Me*.[6]

This search for the divine spark led boomers to follow a number of assorted gurus and religious movements during the Seventies and Eighties. Maharishi Mahesh Yogi, the founder of the Transcendental Meditation Program, gained a wide following in the late '60s with his simplified and popular version of Hindu meditation, which he trademarked under the initials TM. Using the marketplace like a religious version of McDonald's, he courted celebrities such as the Beatles and Mia Farrow.

In 1971 he founded the Maharishi's International University, which is now an accredited university, offering four doctoral programs. Presented as a scientific means to reduce stress, increase productivity, and heighten creativity, TM was taught in some public schools until a federal court in New Jersey ruled that TM was really a religious exercise and could not be taught in its schools. Six million Americans were taught TM and it became the most popular method of meditation that has sprung from Hindu roots.[7]

In January 1991 it was reported in *Rolling Stone* that the Maharishi and the magician Doug Henning had bought 450 acres of Florida property right next to Disneyworld with the intention of creating Veda Land, an amusement park which would offer health food, nonpolluting entertainment, and rides featuring mind-boggling illusions based on Eastern religious teachings.[8]

Other gurus who grabbed national headlines included Swami Muktananda, known as "Baba" to his followers, who taught yoga to such people as former California governor Jerry Brown and singers John Denver and Diana Ross among many others in the Hollywood set. His chief teaching was "God dwells within you as you; worship yourself."

Guru Maharaj Ji at the age of fifteen in 1973 claimed a worldwide following of 6 million. Prominent among his followers, who were called "premises," was Rennie Davis of the Chicago Seven. The founder of the Divine Light Mission, which had 248 centers across the United States, Ji appeared in stadiums across the country where followers fell at his feet as he dispensed "the knowledge" or "divine light."

In 1981 Bhagwan Shree Rajneesh moved his commune in Poona, India, to central Oregon where he bought 64,000 acres of land and created his own community of God. Local residents were outraged when his commune members outvoted them and placed members of their group in city government. Rajneesh was often pictured driving in a new Rolls-Royce down a road lined by his adoring followers who bowed to him as he rode by. A vague image could be seen of him blessing them with a wave of his hand.

His ideal was to create a commune that would be "an experiment in spiritual communism . . . a space where we can create human beings who are not obsessed with comparison, who are not obsessed with the ego, who are not obsessed with personality." But by 1985 the commune was disbanded. Rajneesh was deported, and his followers were doing time for crimes ranging from wiretapping to attempted murder to arson to arranging sham marriages in order to circumvent immigration laws.[9]

Other groups that attracted negative publicity were scientologists, moonies from the Unification Church, and Hare Krishnas, who populated airports in their orange saris and clinking bells as they sought donations from weary travelers. Parents hired deprogrammers to rescue their children from such groups, and books came out describing the "brainwashing" techniques that were used to indoctrinate new devotees.

The appeal of these groups to boomers was that they offered a strong sense of community—a way of life separate from "corrupt" Western society, and they were led by charismatic teachers who seemed to have found enlightenment. One follower of Rajneesh, even after his commune fell apart, said, "I still see him as the wisest person I ever met."[10]

By the mid-'80s when many of these groups were called into question and discredited by the media, it was thought that in some way this grand search for "truth" was over—that boomers would find their way back home to mainline America or that they would give up on religion altogether. Instead of being pictured as devotees to a religious guru, they were seen as addicted to the materialism symbolized by the yuppies. But in 1987 the different segments of Buddhism, Hinduism, the occult, the science of mind, astrology, the teaching of Native American religions, and the belief in extraterrestrials all came together in something called the New Age movement.

In 1987 Jose Arguelles, a professor at Union Graduate School in Colorado, announced that August 16-17, 1987, would mark a new wave of history, the "Harmonic Convergence," a time when a correction would occur in the earth's resonance. In order for this correction to take place, 144,000 people would have to participate to send that vision spontaneously sparking through the imaginations of the majority of humanity. He declared that this was just the start, the opening event in which governments, the military, and polluting industries would be taken apart. By 2010 the earth would be purified and humanity would have found its place in the universal extraterrestrial community.[11]

On that weekend 20,000 New Agers assembled at sacred sites across the country, from Central Park in New York City to Mount Shasta in Northern California, to provide harmony to the world. Participants charged their crystals with the energy of the rising sun, chanted "Ooom," danced and raised their hands in the air, and channeled for ancient ascended masters who told of a new era in human history. Because of a unique lineup of planets in the solar system, Arguelles had persuaded them that this was a high holy day for the world to prepare people for the coming of extraterrestrials who would bring us into the galactic community.

Dr. William Gooch of Hayden Planetarium in Manhattan affirmed the planetary lineup but believed nothing unusual was going on. Perhaps people just wanted to go back to the '60s.[12]

Although it was seen as a great grand joke in the media, later in the year *Time* came out with a cover story on the New Age movement, which talked about the growing number of people attracted to this spiritual quest for enlightenment.

> All in all, the New Age does express a cloudy sort of religion, claiming vague connections with both Christianity and the major faiths of the East (New Agers like to say Jesus spent 18 years in India absorbing Hinduism and the teachings of Buddha), plus an occasional dab of pantheism and sorcery. The underlying faith is a lack of faith in the orthodoxies of rationalism, high technology, routine living, spiritual law-and-order. Somehow, the New Agers believe, there must be some secret and mysterious shortcut or alternative path to happiness and health. And nobody ever really dies.[13]

Although the number of New Agers is hard to come by, John Naisbitt and Patricia Aburdene in *Megatrends 2000* estimate that the number of New Agers ranges between 10 and 20 million Americans.[14] Predominant among New Agers are baby boomers. Lillie Wilson, in the September 1988 issue of *American Demographcis*, says: "New Agers tend to be educated, affluent, and successful people. They are hungry for something that mainstream society has not given them. They say they are looking for 'alternatives,' 'new paradigms,' 'social transformation,' 'personal wholeness,' 'enlightment' and even 'utopia.' And they are willing to pay for it."[15]

New Age Journal, whose subscriptions have increased 900 percent since 1983, states that 91 percent of its subscribers are college educated, with an average household income of nearly $42,000, and a median age of 39.5. The same profile holds for listeners of New Age music, a blend of jazz and meditation music, which Suzanne Doucet in *Billboard* says is "designed to engage the right brain, which evokes intuition, imagination, and altered states of consciousness."[16]

"One third of all age groups say they like New Age music, with the exception of people aged 45 and older (only 23 percent like it)," says Blayne Cutler in a 1989 article in *American Demographics*. "These 16 million New Age fans buy almost $300 million worth of records and tapes a year." The interest in New Age music is second only to pop music, which is liked by 66 percent of the American population.[17]

By looking at these figures we can safely say that 13 to 26 percent of baby boomers are involved in the New Age, almost as many as the 27 percent of boomers who say they are born-again Christians.[18] Numbers do not tell the whole story because New Agers have influence beyond their population. Russell Chandler, religion editor of the *Los Angeles Times*, wrote in his book *Understanding the New Age*:

> New Age influence has indeed touched every facet of contemporary life. Its popularizers and their beliefs are often visible on your television set, at the movies, in printed horoscopes, or at your local health-food store. Even sports and exercise programs, motivational training, psychological counseling, and religious classes are frequent pipelines for New Age thinking.[19]

Andrew Greeley—novelist, priest, and sociologist—reported in a 1984 survey by Chicago's National Opinion Research Council that 42 percent of Americans believe they have been in contact with someone who has died, usually a spouse or sibling. That is up from 27 percent in 1973. In a more recent survey, 63 percent of all adults reported having experienced ESP. Furthermore, 35 percent of Americans reported they had had a mystical experience, "feeling very close to a powerful, spiritual force that seemed to lift you out of yourself."

Greeley said that much of the credit for the rise in reportings of such experiences can be attributed to people such as Shirley MacLaine. Now "millions are less afraid to talk about the experiences." What makes these findings important is not that a majority of Americans report experiencing ESP or other paranormal experiences. What is significant is that "a small minority, maybe under 20 million, have undergone profoundly religious moments of ecstasy. They report out-of-body trips, being bathed in light, or other encounters that transform their lives."[20] Also George Gallup, Jr. reports that 23 percent of Americans, almost one in four, believe in reincarnation, a strong tenet of the New Age.[21]

The core group of New Agers are the ones "we constantly see tending to set trends in America," says John Garrett of the SRI International's Values and Lifestyles program. The trendsetters are what the VALS program calls "Inner-Directeds," a type concentrated in the older half of the baby boom, those who are now nearing or entering their forties. These boomers are saying, "We don't want as many materialistic goods, but the ones we do want have to be quality . . . and they're also going more for the experience of life." Garrett says that in some sense religion represents another diversion. "They don't care for existing religions, so they've come out with a new kind of religion—a New Age one, a kind of attunement."[22]

Religious researchers Bob and Gretchen Passatino say the New Age is "the fastest growing alternative belief system in the country."[23] These beliefs are seen in such mass-market success stories as the *Star Wars* trilogy, with its "let the force be with you" message, and in the 1990 hit *Teenage Mutant Ninja Turtles* and its 1991 sequel *Teenage Mutant Ninja Turtles II* in which Eastern meditation techniques form the backdrop on which all the action takes place. Most interestingly, these movies target the children of boomers who say "Cowabunga, dude," buy Ninja Turtle action figures, and suddenly want pizza instead of hamburgers. When we couple these findings together, we see that rather than being a phenomenon on the sidelines, New Age beliefs and symbols have become a significant part of the belief system of many Americans.

The desire that New Agers express for a spiritual experience is similar in some ways to the worldview of the charismatic movement in Christianity. To be sure, there are differences. While the New Age movement is attractive to college-educated baby boomers, for example, the charismatic movement attracts only 15 percent who are college educated, with 28 percent having some college, 28 percent high school graduates, and 26 percent nongraduates of high school. Charismatic baby boomers also tend to be younger than their New Age counterparts, according to George Gallup.[24] In addition, although charismatic baby boomers have a supernatural worldview that acknowledges the reality of occult practices, the charismatics see themselves in opposition to these practices. Rather than accepting an idea of a oneness of God, they see themselves in a spiritual battle siding with God against the forces of the devil. Exorcisms, speaking in tongues, and physical healings are evidences of the spiritual battle in which Christians are engaged against the forces of evil. Still, as C. Peter Wagner has argued, there is a basic similarity between charismatics and New Agers.

I believe New Agers and charismatics share the same worldview, which is the New Testament worldview that there is supernatural power that generates outside of human existence and human society, but operates through human beings and human social structures, indirectly and sometimes directly. I think both charismatics and the New Age have been on a search for power. So there's no question in the minds of either whether supernatural power is active or not; the question is: What's the source of that power?[25]

Charismatic worship services are much different from those found in mainline and traditional evangelical churches. George Barna, a church consultant, says, "Think about what a traditional church is like. An older person greets you at the door and hands you a mimeographed bulletin. You sit in an uncomfortable pew and stare at the back of someone's head. You sing 400-year-old songs and listen to a 20-minute talk about theology. Then they ask you for money and kick you out."[26]

In contrast, charismatic worship services are an event. Typically, a charismatic service will start with thirty to forty-five minutes of praise singing led by a music group with guitars, piano, and drums. This is followed by a message preached out of the Bible, which sometimes goes way beyond the traditional twenty-minute sermon. Frequently the service concludes when the congregation ministers to each other in prayer, sometimes with healing and exorcisms taking place.

Boomers are flocking to charismatic churches, while mainline denominations are losing members and traditional evangelical churches, such as Southern Baptists and Nazarenes, are holding their own. Charismatic churches are gaining adherents because they emphasize an experience of the Holy Spirit, which causes the believer to be intimately involved in a spiritual battle for the souls of the lost and gives them a personal stake in the results of their faith.

It is this desire for spiritual experience that permeates the life of baby boomers. Whether it is a New Ager seeking a favorite channeler or the charismatic Christian going to a healing seminar, they both hold to the notion that there is more to this life than meets the eye, that beyond this earth is a spiritual world of which they can avail themselves to find meaning and purpose and, more than meaning, a personal experience of salvation. It is to this quest that we now will turn.

Chapter Seven

ADVENTUROUSNESS

The silent retreat at the monastery was quite an experience. For twenty-four hours I was to maintain the discipline of silence. Free from the sounds of television, radio, the telephone, and the voices of other people, I had no choice but to listen to myself and to ask where I was with God.

In the eighteenth hour of the retreat I was outside near a large pond, which was located in the center of the monastery's grounds. When I walked toward the pond, I saw a flock of ducks on the water. As I neared the shore, the ducks quickly swam over to me, expecting to be fed. My hands were empty, so they swam around in circles, glancing at me as though they were disappointed. I said to myself, "Isn't that like the church? If you don't have something to give them, they ignore you."

Suddenly with great excitement the ducks took off in one direction out of my sight. I thought, "Isn't that just like people in the church? As soon as something else comes up they leave." Then a woman appeared on the other side of the pond. In her hands was a package of saltine crackers, and she started throwing them into the water. Appearing out of nowhere the ducks madly dashed to her and playfully ate the crackers and frolicked in the water. I reflected, "Isn't that just like the church? When someone else has something to offer, people will go to them and leave you behind."

Then the woman stopped throwing the crackers into the water. She picked up her things and walked around the pond toward me. I kept my eyes on the water—after all it was a silent retreat and I was not about to break my silence by talking to her. As I was looking out across the water, a package of crackers was thrust into my hands and the woman kept walking. Then God said to me, "I will give you what you need to feed the church." With tears in my eyes I slowly tossed the crackers into the water one by one, and I watched as the ducks frolicked and played as I fed them the bread of life.

No words can adequately explain what that experience of God's presence in my life meant to me. It came at a time when I was wrestling with my ministry in the church and with my relationship with God. It was a spiritual experience, one of many that has made me the believer I am today. At different times in my life, I have had encounters with God that have completely changed the direction of my life. At other times I have felt gentle nudges to do this or that, things that are not readily apparent in their purpose, but when done have been of great benefit. There is nothing static about this relationship to God, it is an ever-changing, ever-deepening, mystical seasoning of my soul. It does not happen by pew sitting on Sunday mornings year after year. It happens when I willingly avail myself and put myself in positions where I can hear the voice of God, when in the blink of an eye my soul can well up with the warm light of God's Spirit.

There is a sense in all of this of being on a spiritual adventure. Not unlike adventurers of old who took off in boats to cross the great oceans to find new lands, the spiritual adventurer crosses the boundaries of the physical world to be touched and moved by forces of the supernatural world beyond the realm of our everyday existence. The spiritual adventurer is not content to sit in a place where his or her soul becomes dormant for lack of attention but seeks the excitement of being challenged to find the source of all life, to feel one's heartbeat when caught up in an experience of the divine.

As baby boomers search for God, what they desire more than anything else is to be part of a spiritual adventure that will challenge them, that will cause them to grow, that will throw off the old and bring in the new, that will engage them with the holiness and sanctity of life, that will put them in places where they will encounter the creative forces of the universe, that will lift them up from the grinding boredom of life to let them know they are unique and important, that their life has meaning and purpose.

People desire to have a mission, an important goal toward which they are working. For example, in the world of work, author Michael Maccoby has identified people who want to make a difference as "self-developers" in *Why Work: Motivating and Leading the New Generation*.

Self-developers make up 25 percent of workers under forty and thirty percent of workers under thirty.[1] These workers are more concerned with opportunities to learn, to grow, and to gain a sense of competency and independence than with moving up in the hierarchy. This is in contrast with experts, who like to provide technical excellence and professional knowledge; helpers, who value relationships and like to respond to people's needs; defenders, who are concerned with survival and the defense of human dignity; and innovators, who enjoy creating and implementing competitive strategy with the goal of winning. Maccoby says:

> But the self-developers are frustrated and turned off by bureaucratic organization and leaders who do not share their values. They resent work that does not allow them to improve their skills and maintain their marketability. They want to be free to respond individually to customers and clients, to be entrepreneurs instead of narrow specialists. They want to be treated as whole persons, not as role performers. Yet they are wary of being swallowed up by work. Motivated to succeed in family life as well as in a career, and to balance work with play, they continually question how much of themselves to invest in the workplace. They want to know why they are working as opposed to expressing themselves outside of the job.[2]

Key concerns that Maccoby brings to our attention are wanting to be "free to respond individually," wanting to be "treated as whole persons, not as role performers," and having a desire to know "why they are working." For them it is not enough just to have a job to support the family. The self-developers who put in eight- to ten- to twelve-hour days want that work to mean something, to be important, to make a difference in this world.

Peter Drucker says in *The New Realities* that knowledge workers are the most important part of the economy. In the industrial age individuals were expendable and easily replaced, but the new pluralist institutions that make up much of our society are organizations of knowledge workers. He says, "Knowledge workers have mobility. They are 'colleagues.' They have both social and economic status. They enjoy the bargaining power that results from social equality and from being economically essential."[3]

The mentality of knowledge workers is similar to that of self-developers in that their chief concern and identity is not tied to the particular business that employs them. It is immaterial to computer specialists whether they work for a hospital, a university, a construction firm, a government agency, or a department store. What matters to them is that the equipment is state of the art and the assignment challenging. This is true for a whole host of workers: the personnel manager, the salesperson, the physical therapist, the accountant, and the doctor. Drucker says, "But their first question is not likely to be: Is it good for the company, or for the hospital, or for the museum? It is more likely to be: Is it professional? . . . Even in the large churches the "professionals"—the music director, or the heads of various "ministries" such as young people or young marrieds—tend to think of themselves first as musicians, youth workers, or marriage counselors, and only secondarily as pastors."[4]

Both of these concepts—the self-developer and the knowledge worker—tie together with what John Naisbitt says is the primary megatrend of the 1990s, the "Triumph of the Individual." Because individuals can leverage change far better than can institutions, the theme for the end of the twentieth century is the supremacy of the individual. After all, it is an individual who creates a work of art, who embraces a philosophy, who starts a new business, who becomes a change agent by inspiring others to succeed, and who has a spiritual experience. "The 1990's are characterized by a new respect for the individual as the foundation of society and the basic unit of change. 'Mass' movements are a misnomer. The environmental movement, the women's movement, the anti-nuclear movement were built one consciousness at a time by an individual persuaded of the possibility of a new reality."[5]

Much of the appeal of the New Age movement is seen in its emphasis on the individual as one who is on a spiritual adventure. In this movement is a nonjudgmental openness to all human experience which accepts other people's experiences as valid without the preconditions of meeting the criteria of some dogma or doctrine. Shirley MacLaine, one of the key spokespersons of the New Age, finds her sources of truth from a wide variety of sources—from Albert Einstein's theory of relativity to astrology, from Buddhism to channelers, from extraterrestrials to the gnostic gospels. Each in its own way has helped form her philosophy of life. Like a spiritual epicurean she collects truths from religions and rites throughout the world to form her own personal view of the cosmos.[6]

J. Z. Knight, another New Ager and friend of MacLaine, the channeler for Ramtha, a 35,000-year-old entity, explains that channeling can be the norm for people "who have been visited by dead relatives and as a result experience God as a warm, all-loving deity rather than a judgmental one." You can find this understanding by acknowledging "that God is inside each individual and that everyone is divine. This outrageous realization creates a human being who no longer echoes the truths, dogmas, and social consciousness of others but starts listening to his or her own opinions."

This brings freedom to individuals because they can "begin living their lives according to what feels right." Through channeling, people come to an expanded awareness "of their own truth," which "sparks our understanding and allows us to evolve to the unlimited potential each person possesses." Knight says,

> Spiritual knowledge is a process that peels away self-imposed limitations. The constant struggle between good and bad is lifted from an individual's soul. People then have the ability to gain extraordinary knowledge and to experience an unlimited life filled with new adventure.[7]

Knight's teaching is appealing to boomers and appalling to traditionalists. Her complete focus is on individuals who through channeling find out they are "divine," who no longer have to echo truths of others but can listen to their own opinions and as a result can "begin living their lives according to what feels right." By doing this they can "experience an unlimited life filled with new adventure."

Of course this brings some questions to mind. What kind of adventure is being offered? Under whose guidance and direction is this adventure going to take place? To whom is the individual held accountable? If all self-imposed limitations are taken away, what will be the glue that holds society together?

These questions are not idle ones, as the results from *The Day America Told the Truth*, a poll taken of Americans in October 1990 by James Patterson and Peter Kim, reveal. In a group of questions that focused on moral authority, they discovered the following:

> So who are our moral leaders now? Well, the overwhelming majority of people (93 percent) said that they—and nobody else—determine what is and what isn't moral in their lives. They base their decisions on their own experience, even on their daily whims.
>
> In addition, almost as large a majority confessed that they would violate the established rules of their religion (84 percent), or that they had actually violated a law because they thought it was wrong in their view (81 percent).

As a result of these findings, Patterson and Kim conclude that "we are a law unto ourselves. We have made ourselves the authority over church and God." They also point out something that ties into New Age demographics: "The fact is that whites are much more likely than others to follow their personal sense of right and wrong. So are Jewish people and Catholics. The same goes for college graduates, liberals, and those earning $45,000 or more a year."[8]

Rather than causing this kind of thinking, the New Age taps into these ideas and gives the believer a certain sense of legitimacy, that indeed "I have the right to choose to do as I believe, not according to the church or to the government, or to any other institution which has failed me in the past. The God-within is my source of truth." Christopher Lasch in an article in *Omni* called "Soul of a New Age" says:

> The New Age movement tries to combine meditation, positive thinking, faith healing, rolfing, dietary reform, environmentalism . . . hypnosis, and any number of other techniques designed to heighten awareness, including elements borrowed from the major religious traditions. But such a concoction, though it can sometimes furnish temporary relief from the symptoms of spiritual distress, cannot bring about the equivalent of a religious conversion, a real change of heart; nor can it bring about even an intellectual conversion to a new point of view capable of standing up against rigorous questioning.
>
> What is missing in the new surrogate religions is spiritual discipline—submission to a body of teachings that has to be accepted even when it conflicts with immediate interests or inclinations and cannot constantly be redesigned to individual specifications.[9]

This clash between two views of spirituality is what differentiates New Agers from the followers of the major religions. Jews follow the Torah, and Christians the Bible, Moslems the Koran, Hindus the Vedas, and Buddhists the Sutras. But New Agers pick and choose as they will from all traditions and add their own twists and turns according to their individual tastes.

I was first exposed to this practice when I took a class on world religions at a junior college. The professor informed us that during Jesus' "missing years"—between the age of twelve and the beginning of his ministry at age thirty—he traveled to India where he learned all his healing powers and spiritual tricks from Tibetan monks. Although no historical evidence supports this, it is a widely accepted thought in the New Age movement. Its chief teacher is Elizabeth Clare Prophet, the leader of the Church Universal and Triumphant, which has an estimated 10,000 to 25,000 members across the United States. Her books, such as *The Lost Years of Jesus* and *The Lost Teaching of Jesus*, are found on college campuses across the United States. In 1988 she was on a tour when she came to Southern California. Wanting to find out more about the New Age movement, I went to hear her speak at a seminar in a Long Beach hotel.

As I entered the hotel conference room, my eyes were immediately drawn to the front where a twenty-five-foot wide altar had been constructed. On the altar was an odd assortment of articles: two menorahs with their seven candles, large crystals, a green emerald, four purple flower arrangements, and a perfect twenty-inch Statue of Liberty.

On the floor in front of the altar was a thirty-inch statue of the Hindu Siva god. Behind the altar on the wall were three large pictures: on the left a picture of Jesus, in the center a picture of the threefold Divine Self, and on the right a picture of someone called St. Germain.

As I sat in my chair I looked at the other five hundred people who had come for this session. It looked like almost any middle-class congregation—young and old, racially mixed, casual clothes, and hopeful looks.

Suddenly a hush came over the room as Elizabeth Clare Prophet arrived, dressed completely in white with a blood-red amethyst resting on the nape of her neck. In a subdued singsong voice she intoned something to the effect of, "Welcome to the teaching of the New Age." Then she gave an invocation to the seven archangels, which finished with "Father, Son, Holy Spirit, and Divine Mother" as she gave the Catholic sign of the cross with an added movement at the end.

She followed this by inviting the audience to open up their "Mantras of the Ascended Masters for the Initiation of the Chakras" book and asked us to sing number 46. To my astonishment the familiar tune of "Holy, Holy, Holy" was played through the speaker system, but the words sang the praises of Michael, the Prince of the Archangels.

As voices rang out with these unfamiliar words, I could feel a cold chill going down my neck. This was not some hokey, New Age mumbo jumbo that only attracted people on the fringes of society. This was something that was taken very seriously by those around me. Their singing was much more passionate than the singing in many Christian churches I have attended. As a Christian I was very uncomfortable with the mixture of familiar music with words that were far afield from Christian doctrine.

Throughout the five-hour lecture a bewildering number of teachings were given, which culminated in a rendition of Ave Maria followed by a channeled message from St. Germain speaking through Elizabeth Clare Prophet. The seminar was capped by an invitation to come forward, during which people in the audience were blessed as Prophet placed an emerald on their foreheads.

Russell Chandler, religion writer for the *Los Angeles Times* and author of *Understanding the New Age*, says of Prophet, "As the 'Vicar of Christ', she claims to be God's chosen earthly messenger for direct dictations (channeled messages) from a host of ascended masters including Buddha, Jesus, Saint Germain, Pope John XXIII, Merlin the Magician, Christopher Columbus, and K-17, the 'head of the Cosmic Secret Service.' . . . Prophet says she has had 'a very profound calling from Jesus.'[10]

As I went away from the seminar I was disturbed by the curious mix of occultism, spiritualism, and gnosticism, sprinkled with elements of Christian music, all of which produced a powerful spiritual experience in the audience but one I would not recommend. It was distinctly anti-Christian, as well as anti-Hindu, and anti-Buddhist. Even as mantras, which were taken from Buddhist forms of worship, were chanted, I had the feeling that, like the Christian songs, they too had been changed to fit the teachings and to give support to the message that was given.

The New Age movement has two separate branches. One is the pop movement, which gets the attention, the channelers and the oc-cultists. The other is a more serious look at human society. *New Age Journal* editor Florence Graves says, "Unfortunately, the pop phe-nomenon is overshadowing something that is very real and pretty important." Saying that her magazine covers the less sensationalistic aspects of New Age thinking, such as ethical investing, organic food, holistic health, and mind/body awareness, she says, "All these subjects represent parts of an impulse that is genuine and involves significant numbers of people."[11]

Another publisher, Eric Utne of the *Utne Reader* says, "It makes me nervous—all the channeling, the crystals . . . but I think there's a parallel interest in social activism developing out there, too. I think these two strands are beginning to flourish in both salutary and repug-nant ways."[12]

Ralph Blum, author of *The New Book of Runes: A Handbook for the Use of an Ancient Oracle, the Viking Runes*, points out that one aspect of the New Age movement is a desire to get back one's own power. He feels that runes are totally non-occult and do not have any power in and of themselves. Instead he sees the use of the stones, through which ancient Vikings consulted the gods for answers to daily problems, as a Jungian tool which allows people to access data from the unconscious. As a result he gets many letters from psychiatrists and counselors who use runes as a diagnostic tool.[13]

Ralph White teaches at New York City's Open Center and offers courses and workshops to brokers on Wall Street on such subjects as "Aspects of Zen practice," "internal kung fu," and "Jungian sym-bolism in astrology." He echoes Blum's sentiments that the New Age movement is a serious endeavor for those who are searching for truth.

We see this movement as a different perspective on life, a holistic view of life. It encompasses an enormous spectrum involving the body, mind, and spirit, including an increased awareness of nutrition, the rise in ecological thinking, a change in business perspectives, greater emphasis on preventive medicine, a shift to Jungian psychology, an emphasis on the individual's intuition. Many people see themselves as living in a pretty meaningless world, and there is a profound cry for meaning. We've seen that tendency in churches, because the way religion is presented traditionally has spoken to our inner selves less and less. People want a living, feeling experience of spirituality. They yearn to get in touch with the soul.[14]

Marilyn Ferguson in her landmark book, *The Aquarian Conspiracy*, which some have called the bible of the New Age, interviewed 185 people whom she had identified as being persons engaged in social transformation in many different areas of our culture. These people were leaders in education, science, business, law, the arts, and government. They were the tip of the iceberg of millions who were involved in something she called "The Aquarian Conspiracy," a leaderless but powerful network that was working to bring about powerful change in the United States. She says, "This network is the Aquarian Conspiracy. It is a conspiracy without a political doctrine. Without a manifesto. With conspirators who seek power only to disperse it, and whose strategies are pragmatic, even scientific, but whose perspective sounds so mystical that they hesitate to discuss it."[15]

What was the nature of this mysticism? The respondents to Ferguson's questions considered the following spiritual disciplines and growth modalities to be the most important in their own spiritual development: Zen, 40 percent; yoga 40 percent; Christian mysticism, 31 percent; journals and dream journals, 31 percent; psychosynthesis, 29 percent; Jungian therapy, 23 percent; Tibetan Buddhism, 23 percent; transcendental meditation, 21 percent; Sufism, 19 percent; and transactional analysis, 11 percent.

When asked if they accepted psychic phenomena and the transpersonal dimension as a reality, choosing from a spectrum of belief from strongly sure to disbelieving, they tended to believe (strongly or moderately sure) in telepathy, 96 percent; psychic healing, 94 percent; precognition, 89 percent; clairvoyance, 88 percent; psychokinesis, 82 percent; cosmic intelligence, 86 percent; consciousness that survives bodily death, 76 percent; and reincarnation, 57 percent. She says "a number protested the use of the word *belief*, saying that they had accepted these phenomena because of direct experience."[16] When asked about their earlier religious background, 55 percent said Protestant; 22 percent Judaic; 18 percent Catholic; 2 percent other; and 5 percent none. Most startling of all, 81 percent said they were no longer active in the religion of their childhood.[17]

This turning away from a Judeo-Christian worldview to a new paradigm that sees "humankind embedded in nature" is as much a failure of the church to provide an authentic Christian spirituality as it is anything else. For most traditions of the Christian faith the goal is pretty much the same. For evangelicals it is for a person to be "converted." For charismatics it is to experience the "second birth" and to "speak in tongues." For Catholics it is to be "confirmed." For mainline Protestants it is to become a "member." Because this process is so familiar to us, it is not seen as being very spiritual, but when looked at from another point of view we see something else.

Frank Trippett, in "The Hesse Trip," a *Look* article published in 1971, found that his Christian upbringing was not so different from Eastern religious practices as one might think.

> Of course, I had the advantage of being reared in a sect that drilled me in esoteric things, convincing me that by being properly immersed in water, for example, I would be instantly reborn and would in fact live forever. They taught me that if I munched a bit of cracker and swallowed a tiny draught of grape juice, I would come into instant communion with the all-knowing power of existence—an all-knowing power, that, incidentally, was utterly singular while at the same time divided into three parts. They drilled in the teachings of the sect's ranking hero, and in this lore I learned among other things, that I would gain myself by losing myself. Although my sect, as far as I recall, never used the *I Ching*, it taught that I could seek answers from the beyond itself by falling on my knees, by speaking to that singular great power in any or all of his three parts. I grew up, of course, in the remote and mystical and impenetrable American South, and was reared there in a congregation of the Southern Baptist Church.[18]

When we strip Christianity away from Western materialistic rationality, we do not find the "Historical Jesus." Instead we find an individual who engaged in some rather unscientific activities. He walked on water, cast out demons, healed the sick, fed the five thousand, calmed the sea, was resurrected from the dead, and appeared to the disciples in a body that was not of this earth. Far from being respectable, he associated with tax collectors and prostitutes, had no place to lay his head, had a somewhat suspect birth, and preached against the religious authorities of his time.

To his followers he promised the gift of the Holy Spirit and eternal life if they believed in him. He also told them that after his death he would come back again. Jesus was not a quiet guru trying to find truth in calm contemplation nor was he a defender of stale ritual. His life was the ultimate spiritual adventure, which went from birth to death to life again in the resurrection.

The irony for the baby boom generation is that by the time the good news got to them, it had been watered down by so much tradition and rationalized by so many theologians and spewed forth by so many uninspired preachers that its power to transform lives was buried under hundreds of years of dogma and doctrine that covered up its radical spirituality.

So the goal of the church was to get members and converts, not to change lives. The goal became respectability and conformity to society, rather than challenge to the status quo, which winked at inequality and ignored spirituality. The winners were those who knew the right doctrine and could rattle off the right scriptures at the appropriate time when their role as the Reverend demanded it.

To those who desired an experience of God, who wanted to do something more than serve on committees or to usher on Sundays, who wanted to go beyond an oath of membership to the religious club, Christianity was found to be severely lacking in integrity and compassion. What boomers longed for was an authentic experience of the power and love of this Jesus so many people had talked about. But instead of just talking about it, they wanted to live it.

The dissatisfaction of people with the North American church was registered in a 1989 George Gallup poll. Gallup found that while 51 percent defined faith as a relationship to God, only 4 percent equated it with membership in a church. When asked, "Do you think a person can be a good Christian or Jew without going to church or synagogue?" 76 percent of Americans said yes, with 81 percent in the West answering in the affirmative.[19] Fifty-nine percent of Americans said that churches were too concerned with organizational matters, and 31 percent said that most churches and synagogues did not have a clear sense of the real spiritual nature of religion.[20]

In November 1989, a *Psychology Today* article, "The Empty Church Syndrome," reported that the acceptance of religious teaching by the unchurched is surprisingly high. Three-quarters of those surveyed believe that Jesus is God or the Son of God and say they pray quite often to God. Instead of going to church, their busy lifestyles are focused on having time for themselves, their friends, and family, who give them the spiritual enrichment they do not find in church. Almost one in four of the unchurched say they have turned away from the church in search of a deeper spiritual meaning.[21]

The fact that people are turning away from the church in search of deeper spiritual meaning says at least as much about the church as about the people who are turning away. The picture that comes through in all of this is one of the church as a nice place to go to see friends and to have fellowship, but not as a place to be challenged in faith or with being a good Christian. What is lacking is a connection between going to church and developing a stronger faith in God.

This is most clearly seen when we look at Americans and their belief in the Bible. While 80 percent of Americans believe the Bible is the literal or inspired Word of God, only 40 percent would turn to it first to test their religious beliefs. When asked how often they read the Bible, Americans reported that 33 percent read it at least once a week (15 percent daily) and 12 percent once a month; 50 percent say they read the Bible less than once a month, of which 24 percent say they never read it.

Even though a high percentage believe in the importance of the Bible, many do not know what it says. Only 40 percent knew that Jesus delivered the Sermon on the Mount, and less than 50 percent could name the four Gospels. This was true across all educational levels, including those who had graduated from college. Thirty-three percent of all teenagers, and 20 percent of teenagers who attend religious services did not know why Easter was celebrated.[22] This lack of understanding of even the basic beliefs of the Christian faith and the lack of biblical knowledge show that for the most part the church in America has done a woefully inadequate job of teaching the Christian faith, much less converting people to be believers.

Underlying this is the assumption by many Christian leaders that this is a Christian nation and all they have to do is open church doors and people will show up. Others think what is missing is not Christian spirituality but the right methods. Thus pastors flock to church growth seminars across the land, hoping to find the right fix for their church so it can be one that is actually growing. What is missing from much of this discussion about the failures of the Christian church in America is the idea of spirituality and the realization that what boomers want from their churches is not less, but more.

Churches who take seriously the desire for an authentic Christian spirituality, who understand boomers' need for self-fulfillment, who do not see visitors as potential members but instead as people to be discipled, who realize that believers want to go way beyond the vows of membership to find their own ministry, who offer an adventure of faith—these are the churches who are reaching the baby boom.

Bill Hybels, founder and senior pastor of Willow Creek Community Church outside of Chicago, the second largest Protestant church in America, with a congregation of over 15,000 on weekends, did a community survey in the summer of 1975. The biggest complaint people had with the church was that "the church is always pleading for my money."

Based on his marketing survey, Hybels started his church using a unique approach. On Sundays he offers a "seeker service" using drama, music, and relevant Bible-based messages for seekers who do not have to say anything, sing anything, sign anything, or give anything. These worship services are what he calls "Christianity 101 and 201." On Wednesday evenings the church offers another worship service called "New Community," which is for born-again Christians. He calls this service "Christianity 301 and 401," and it offers corporate worship and meatier teaching to challenge believers to grow in their faith in Jesus Christ.[23]

At a seminar on "Reaching the Unchurched in the 1990s," Hybels talked about the importance of helping believers find their ministry. His church has an extensive program that enables new believers to identify their spiritual gifts, their spiritual passions, and their personality types. Spiritual gifts are found in the Bible and range from teaching to leadership to helping to hospitality. These are given to believers through the Holy Spirit.

Spiritual passions have to do with what makes your heart beat fast for ministry. Do you get excited about working with youth or children, teaching a Bible study to adults, or being in mission to the poor in the inner city? What do you get enthused about when you think of ministry?

Using the Myers/Briggs Personality Test, believers are then encouraged to find out their personality type. For example, a person may have a gift for teaching and have a spiritual passion for working with young adults, but may be an introvert. Instead of leading a Bible study for young adults, this person might be better suited to writing and preparing the materials that will be taught by someone who has the same spiritual gift and the same spiritual passion but is an extrovert who loves to be in front of people.[24]

Rick Warren, who started the Saddleback Valley Community Church in 1980 in Orange County, California, began his church after knocking on 500 doors in the community and asking residents what they wanted in a church. Four complaints about church kept recurring in his survey: One, sermons are boring, not relevant; two, members are unfriendly to visitors; three, most churches are more interested in your money than in you as a person; and four, quality child care is a necessity.

As part of his outreach Warren developed the Saddleback Strategy, which is prominently displayed in the church bulletin. It states: "We emphasize relationships, not organized religion. . . . We offer you friendliness, openness, and unconditional love. This is a place to grow. . . . We're more interested in building up people than building facilities. . . . We offer a style of music and worship that is culturally relevant."

On the church's registration card, which people are encouraged to fill out, are two interesting categories, "members" and "attenders." What is the difference? Members are people in the church who have a ministry, whether it is teaching Sunday school, playing in the church orchestra, leading small groups, or being part of a visiting team. Attenders are those who attend worship, maybe as often as every week, but have not yet defined their ministry in the church. At the church's tenth anniversary worship service, Warren said they had 1,400 members involved in all kinds of ministries. Their average worship attendance was around 4,000, and in 1989 more than 9,000 people attended the Easter worship service.

How successful has this approach been? *Church Growth Today* ranks Saddleback as the fastest growing church in Orange County and the twelfth fastest growing church in America. Another important factor in all this is the fact that Saddleback is a Southern Baptist church. You would not know the denomination by the congregation's appearance or by the worship service, as most of the songs are written by members of the church. But its underlying doctrines contain all the beliefs of the Southern Baptist denomination. Of his approach to reaching the unchurched, most of whom are baby boomers, Warren says, "We accept people as they are. This is a place to grow, not a place for perfect people who have it all together."[25]

What Willow Creek and Saddleback take seriously is the need of people to be in ministry. These churches do not think that only clergy have a calling. Each believer is seen as a child of God who has a special set of gifts and passions, which—when mixed with a certain kind of personality—makes that person uniquely qualified to do his or her ministry.

Vineyard Christian Fellowship in Anaheim, California, which was started by John Wimber in 1977, struggled for the first two years with the gifts of the Holy Spirit. After a twenty-week series of messages about God's healing power, they were disappointed because as they prayed for people, still nothing happened. It was not until May 1979 that God visited the church in a mighty way and they began to experience God's power. Wimber says, "Our large and small gatherings are characterized by things that I had known about only from history books. Quaking, shaking, falling under the power of God and the public exercise of spiritual gifts such as words of knowledge and prophecy are commonplace."

In the first five years of the church, membership went from zero to 3,000. By 1990 the church was serving thousands each Sunday, and over 300 Vineyard Christian Fellowship Congregations were spread across the country with over 100,000 followers. The church is primarily made up of baby boomers who were reared in a mainline church. More recently, followers have been coming from traditional evangelical churches.[26] Most have had some kind of religious background. Wimber calls them "religious refugees" who make up part of a nation of "believers who do not belong." Of his approach to ministry, which is called "power evangelism," he says:

Today in America there is a tremendous increase in the occult, spiritualism and all sorts of demonic activity. In their search for spiritual reality, people are seeking new modes of religious thought. The West is looking to the East for a faith.

We believe that Jesus ministered in power to the total person. His message was not for the mind alone; it was also for the spirit and body. Jesus preached, taught, and healed. . . . People in our culture need to see that God is more powerful than the lifestyles they are serving. We are discovering that scripturally defined signs and wonders are playing a major role in getting the gospel message out to a nation that needs help and spiritual direction.

But our ministry style does not flow directly from the prewar models of the faith healers. We are a body ministry. Men and women alike have the power and authority to pray for the sick and to minister in all the spiritual gifts. Some are more adept than others, but no one is exempt. The ministry is for everyone.[27]

Wimber's approach to ministry has drawn fire from church leaders of all persuasions, but one thing he has in common with churches that are reaching the baby boom is that he takes spirituality seriously and he teaches believers how to put their faith into action. A number of seminars, conferences, and classes are continually being taught for believers who want to learn to do it themselves.

Churches do not have to be megachurches or have members in the thousands to do this. Holliston United Methodist Church in Pasadena, California, completely turned around in the late 1980s when it encouraged a couple of baby boomers who had a vision of sending a work team to Kenya. A scouting party returned from Kenya and reported a great need at a Methodist hospital that had no water. Surprisingly, when this was brought to the attention of the congregation, it was discovered that in the congregation were a number of engineers experienced in water and sewage projects. All the designing and planning could be done by the church itself.

Through these efforts the congregation has sent numerous work teams to Kenya. The teams have been made up of members of the Holliston Church and members of other churches throughout Southern California. They have put in a water system and a sewage system, helped to dig wells, and set up a dental clinic at a Methodist hospital, which is now ministering to thousands of needy people in that country. They have raised hundreds of thousands of dollars from a wide variety of sources to do this work.

Now attendance and membership are up at Holliston. There are children in the Sunday school, and the congregation has new life because the people now see themselves in mission beyond their doors. By giving some boomers with a vision permission to be in ministry, the whole church is caught up in a spiritual adventure. These Christians can see their faith being put into action. In this ministry of helping the poor and the hungry, God's love has become real and alive in a brand-new way.

Steve Petty, the pastor of Holliston when the Kenya project was put in motion, says the key event that started the church on a new track took place in September 1985 when he gave a revivalistic message that demanded an altar call. Petty says: "I asked for members of the church who wanted to rededicate their life to the Christian faith to join me at the altar. I went to the altar and knelt to pray. I was not sure what happened, but when I turned around, every member of the congregation except one had joined me to renew their life in Christ. That was a spiritual event. That was when the whole attitude and life of the church turned around. The Holy Spirit began to work in our church in a totally new way."[28]

It was at that same altar seventeen years before that I had given my life to Christ and had begun my spiritual adventure. Now my home church is experiencing its own revival and has found new life because the individual Christians have been released to be in ministry. Although by some standards it is a small church of 230 members, its impact has reached far beyond the doors of the church, as it is in ministry to the world.

What the New Age and Christian churches that are reaching the baby boom have in common is an understanding that spirituality encompasses all of life. Both go beyond the Greek model of mind separated from body and focus on the Hebrew ideal of the soul, which encompasses the whole being and essence of each person. This religious mindset is not afraid to ask believers to see the totality of their life—work, play, God, family, and individuality—as one complete whole, which is affected by all of its parts.

These movements seek to integrate the person, to refine and mold that person in the image of their God. To be sure, there are significant differences between New Age and a truly Christian spirituality, but the church cannot afford to ignore the central point: Baby boomers today are in search of a spiritual adventure of discovery and revelation which will challenge them to become more like God and will empower them to be better human beings.

3
THE FUTURE

Imagine there's no heaven;
It's easy if you try;
No hell below us;
Above us only sky.
Imagine all the people
Living for today.

Imagine there's no countries;
It isn't hard to do;
Nothing to kill or die for
And no religion too.
Imagine all the people
Living life in peace.

You, you may say I'm a dreamer.
But I'm not the only one.
I hope some day you will join us
And the world will be as one. . . .

Chapter Eight

Millennialism

The year 2000 has stood as a beacon for all of humanity during this century. This watershed year will mark the beginning of a new millennium, the next thousand years of human history reaching to the year 3000. It also stands as a tantalizing goal for our earth: It is as if making it to the year 2000 guarantees hope for the future.

The reason this seems to be such an impossible goal is because of the apocalyptic nature of our century. Since 1900 we have seen the holocaust of Armenians in Turkey, of Jews in Germany, of Russians in the Soviet Union, of Chinese by Communists during the Chinese Revolution, of Cambodians by the Khmer Rouge, and of Kurds by the Iraqi army. No country, no region of the world has been left untouched by the violence that has typified our century.

Two world wars put the whole world in jeopardy, and since the dropping of the first nuclear bomb on Hiroshima in 1945, the world has been living under the threat of nuclear annihilation. In twenty minutes, with the release of the nuclear weapons of Russia and the U.S., the world as we know it could be devastated and civilization ended.

Even as the Russian revolution takes its course, a large number of its weapons remain. At one point during the coup attempt in August 1991, the conspirators seized the briefcase that contained Gorbachev's codes to launch nuclear weapons. How close the world was to a nuclear exchange or a horrendous mistake that would kill millions, we will never know.

Boomers, all of whom have been born since the birth of the bomb in 1945, have been living in the epoch of fear, for they have been all too aware that at any moment they could be blown away in the first salvos of World War III or could die a lingering death from the aftereffects of nuclear radiation. Chellis Glendinning in *Waking up in the Nuclear Age* says:

Before I wove the nuclear threat into my personal story, I had no concept of the effect of nuclear weapons on my life. As I explored the question, I realized two points: one, as a Baby Boomer, I had never known a world without nuclear weapons; and two, I had lived my entire life incapable of planning for the future. A perfect expression of the Be Here Now generation, I never seem to think more than a few weeks or months ahead. Now that I have identified this future uncertainty, I am finally able to imagine a future for myself, even though I admit, consciously for the first time, that it might not come to be.[1]

The dark cloud of nuclear annihilation has been a constant companion for those born in the nuclear age. During the '50s schoolchildren were drilled in nuclear preparedness. During air raid drills they were taught to cover their heads as they cowered in the hallways of schools across the land in the anticipation of a nuclear attack. During the Cuban Missile Crisis they helped their parents prepare for "the big one" by stocking up on food and they watched the building of bomb shelters in their backyards.

Who could forget the *Twilight Zone* episode in which neighbors go to war over who is going to stay in a bomb shelter during an apparent nuclear attack? The image of one family's being inside the shelter while neighbors banged on the outside and begged to be let in, is firmly imprinted in my mind.

The lesson of the nuclear age is that war is not "out there" somewhere: Death can be visited on any neighborhood in the world. During the opening scenes of the Gulf War, we watched in horror as SCUD missiles indiscriminately landed in Israel and in Saudi Arabia. We saw Israeli citizens and Saudi civilians clamp gas masks on their faces to protect themselves from a possible chemical blast. Much of the rationale of going into that war was to keep Saddam Hussein from developing and delivering nuclear weapons.

In modern war, no one is immune. No one is safe. Movies such as *Dr. Strangelove, Failsafe, The Day After, Testament, Terminator 2*, and books such as *On the Beach* and *Warday* bring home the disturbing message that all it takes is one mistake, one crazy person, or one fouled up government decision by either side of the nuclear equation and the world could be blown up. One mushroom cloud of mass destruction would stand as a testimony to humankind's ability to destroy itself.

As a teenager I remember going to see *The Planet of the Apes*, a very popular movie with boomers. In it, Charlton Heston's spaceship ends up on a planet ruled by apes. Heston's character meets humans who have become the slaves of the apes. His only hope is to find his spaceship so he can escape the planet and go back to earth. In the last scene of the movie, Heston is riding a horse on a beach as he comes upon a disturbing sight. In anger and despair he exclaims, "Those maniacs—they did it!" As the scene unfolds we see the Statue of Liberty buried in the sand. The planet of the apes was Earth. Heston had made it home to a world that had blown itself up.

What now seems like a somewhat silly series of movies was one that brought home to boomers the futility of living in the nuclear age. In sequels to the movie, nuclear weapons were a key element. One movie revolved around a group of nuclear survivors who lived in bombed-out New York City. They worshiped a nuclear bomb as a religious icon that promised salvation to its believers. Its symbolic relation to a policy dubbed MAD (Mutual Assured Destruction) by the government did not go unnoticed in the psyche of the baby boom generation.

For the most part boomers have had an ambivalent relationship with the future. It has not been something they have looked forward to or planned for. Anything beyond A.D. 2000 seems eons away. If you talk to boomers about planning for their retirement or about Social Security, you usually get a blank expression and a remark such as, "Social Security will be long gone before I get there." This negative outlook affects the way they look at the environment ("We'll all be wearing gas masks."), education ("We're raising a generation of illiterates."), the family ("We will all be living alone."), and religion ("The church will be dead.").

Much of this attitude can be credited to living life in the nuclear age. First, unlike generations who went before them, boomers have no guarantee of a future. For the first time in history, humanity has in its hands the means by which to destroy the earth. This has nothing to do with superstition, religion, or theory—the destruction of Hiroshima assured us of that. Letting loose the nuclear genie has put the world in great peril. In the blink of an eye, mass destruction can rain down on the earth and wipe out the human race.

Unlike generations before them who saw themselves as passing on the baton of culture to the next generation, boomers have viewed themselves as the last generation. If another generation is to follow, there is a hesitation about passing on a culture that has brought the world to the precipice of annihilation.

Second, instead of being the savior of world, technology is seen by many as the destroyer of the earth. For many it makes much better sense to go back to the earth, to eat natural foods, to eat lower down on the food chain, and to embrace Mother Earth. The animal rights movement and the environmental movement are reactions to the polluting effects of the industrial age. For persons involved in these movements the epitome of technology gone mad is the nuclear bomb.

Third, with no assured future, boomers live for the now, for the present, for the moment. Long-range plans seem futile and irrelevant. What is important is to make it today. After all, why save for the future if there is not going to be one? Why not build up a big deficit, if we are never going to have to pay it off? Why think about being with someone for fifty years, if the world is going to end in ten?

Fourth, and most important, the dominant view of the future is apocalyptic: The end of the world is at hand. Strangely enough, both New Agers and Christian fundamentalists embrace this view. Annie Gottlieb writes:

> It's fascinating that the two groups of adults most obsessed with the apocalypse are right-wing fundamentalists and the Sixties generation. Each group believes the other is the party of the Devil. . . . Born again friends point out the many signs of the prophesied Last Days: Whitley Strieber, in *Nature's End*, calls these the "sunset years" before ecological or nuclear disaster. One faction speaks of "the Last Judgment," the other of "humanity's final exam." Christian fundamentalists have their Book of Revelation, the greatest disaster epic ever penned; . . . our generation seems determined to rival it, for our most characteristic artifact is the apocalyptic fantasy.[2]

This apocalyptic view of the future is found in many different sources. The best-selling book since 1970, with over 25 million copies in print, is a 180-page paperback with the startling title *The Late Great Planet Earth* written by Hal Lindsey. With its end-of-the-world motif, this book has proved to be a perfect match for boomers who expect the end to come at any moment.

In the pages of his book, Lindsey painted a picture of the last judgment according to his interpretation of the Book of Revelation and apocalyptic prophecies found in the Old Testament. Central to this scenario was the founding of Israel in 1948, which was seen as one of the key signs leading to the Second Coming of Christ within a generation. Because a generation in the Bible is something like forty years, Lindsey said Christ would return by 1988, during the lifetime of the baby boom generation.[3]

Another key event surrounding the Second Coming would be the reemergence of a new Roman Empire. This reemergence is seen in the Common Market and the move toward the unification of Europe. According to Lindsey, this may be the same as the ten-nation confederacy predicted by Daniel and the Book of Revelation.[4]

After the establishment of a unified Europe, a dictator would arise from this federation of nations to lead the world. This dictator would be none other than the antichrist. Along with this would be the establishment of a one-world religion and a one-world economic system. Also the United States would be aligned with Europe and would by this time have lost its position as leader of the free world.

The final event, according to Lindsey, would be the joining together of Russia, identified as "Gog" in the Bible, and the Arab states, which would attack Israel. By an act of God these forces would be destroyed and Israel would come to believe in the true Messiah. This would be the last war of history, involving all the nations of the world, during which Christ would return to prevent the total destruction of humankind.[5]

All these events would take place in a seven-year period marked by the rule of the antichrist. Of this period Lindsey warned that there would be no advantage to being alive. On the stage of world history, this would be the greatest holocaust brought about by the cruelest tyrant of all time.[6]

But would everyone have to suffer? Lindsey said no, that there was a way out. You did not have to be here during the seven years of tribulation. According to Lindsey's interpretation of the Bible there would be one generation which would never know death. Of this generation, those who believed in Jesus Christ would escape the great tribulation, the worst bloodshed, disease, and starvation the world would ever know.[7]

How would they avoid the tribulation? Through the "rapture," the ultimate trip, which offers the promise of three great miracles. First, believers would not die; instead they would be snatched up from earth to be with Jesus. Second, they would miss the tribulation and only return to earth with Christ after the seven-year period of darkness. Third, with Christ they would help usher in the new millennium, a period of 1,000 years during which believers would repopulate the earth under the rule of Christ. At the end of this millennial period, unbelievers would lead a rebellion against Christ and then Christ would create a new heaven and a new earth.[8]

In the '70s boomers fully embraced this view of prophecy, and cars were covered with bumper stickers such as the one that said: "Watch out! If the Rapture comes, this car will be empty." *A Thief in the Night*, a popular movie about the rapture, portrayed believers being snatched up out of cars, showers, and the United States Congress without warning, leaving the rest of the world to wonder what had happened to their friends and neighbors.

This view of a great escape from the problems of the world proved to be a perfect match for a generation that did not want to grow up. What better answer for fears about death and nuclear war than the one Lindsey proposed? Through the rapture a believer would be beamed up like a character from *Star Trek* and would get to watch the events of the tribulation from the safety of heaven. After the horrible events were over, the believer would return to a world ruled by Christ. This solution offered no mess, no fuss, and best of all, no suffering.

Although 1988 has come and gone, this view of the future is a common one among the baby boom generation. As Europe unites in 1992, as the world economic system becomes more and more interrelated, and as the year 2000 approaches, this view is one that will retain its popularity. It is not unusual to hear boomers say, "I believe Jesus will return in my lifetime."

Hal Lindsey is not alone in his portrayal of the apocalyptic future. In *Herald of the New Age*, Ruth Montgomery, an influential writer of the New Age movement, postulates that a prophecy by Nostradamus will come true in July, September, or October 1999. This prophecy was confirmed by Edgar Cayce when he "spoke in trance of a shifting of the poles near the end of the century and of radical changes in seasons, together with the rising or sinking of land areas all over the globe. . . . This global catastrophe, the Guides claim, will cleanse the earth of pollution and evil people and will usher in the long-awaited New Age of a thousand years of peace."[9]

Whereas Montgomery sees a polar shift in 1999 which will precede a new millennium of peace, Jose Arguelles, the initiator of the Harmonic Convergence, sees the Solar Age coming about as a result of humanity's resonating with earth's electromagnetic battery.

People will enter into a period he calls post-history. They will live as New Maya when the New Age begins. This New Age will come about when everyone on earth takes part in utilizing Earth's electromagnetic battery. This will happen in 2012 and is dependent upon the full participation of every last organism upon the planet.

The summons to be part of this galactic entrainment comes from the sun itself, which the Egyptians called Ra, the Supreme Solar Lord.[10] By 1992 emissaries of the sun will be among us, preparing for the establishment of the kingdom of heaven on earth.[11]

Also in 1992, small groups of humans will begin to gather into extended family units to locate and align themselves with planetary points to augment the coming resonance with the earth. These communities will set up solar temples which will be used for contemplation and energy regeneration. Computer technology will be combined with solar energy to provide houses of senses which will enable people to tune into the electromagnetic battery of the earth.

The long-term results of this will be the improvement of sensual enjoyment along with the equal improvement of the capacity for psychic powers. As a result, everyone will be a medium, a channel, which will allow all persons to experience psychic power beyond their wildest dreams.[12]

Arguelles also sees the importance of divesting the old military establishment of its wealth and power, and cleaning up toxic facilities, as being an integral part of the Harmonic Convergence. The ability to establish the Solar Age rests on divesting ourselves of unnecessary military power and the production of wasteful and toxic consumer goods.[13]

A new government will be put in place led by the High Council of Solar-Planetary Affairs, which will monitor the alignment of the terrestrial electromagnetic battery with the solar frequencies and pulsations to insure the greater harmonic resonance of the whole. The decisions of this council will naturally affect all other actions on the planet.[14]

Arguelles sees a great change taking place over the next generation. Earth will abandon war and be awakened to a higher purpose through the Campaign for the Earth. The final five-year period from 2007 to 2012 will be critical as galactic synchronization crews take their places at all the planetary light-body nodes.

Then the unique moment will take place, the closing of the Great Cycle. The evolutionary interim of homo sapiens will finish its course to be replaced by our entry into the Galactic Federation. The Ancestors, the Elders and Saints, the Maya returned, our deepest selves, Time and Space, will all be made one. A new adventure will begin.[15]

As fanciful as this may seem, Arguelles can point to the events that have shaken the world since the Harmonic Convergence in 1987. The reunification of Germany, the fall of communism in Eastern Europe, and the Russian Revolution of August 1991—all signal a great change taking place in our world.

Those troubled by his missionary zeal should keep in mind that most religions seek converts. Arguelles' evangelism is no less strident than Bill Bright's "I Found It" campaign in the 1970s which sought to convert the world to Christianity so Christ would come again. Although the term *harmonic convergence* sounds so peaceful, it is based on apocalyptic events, especially for those who are part of the old world order.

Although Lindsey and Montgomery and Arguelles come at this from different points of view (Lindsey the fundamentalist Christian and Montgomery and Arguelles New Agers), the point is similar. Before the millennium, whether it be the Christian vision of a heaven on earth ruled by Christ or the New Age ushered in by extraterrestrials and spirit guides, there will be a period of disaster, whether it is Armageddon, a natural catastrophe, or the collapse of the old order.

Of course this is nothing new. Whole religions have been built on the premise that the world is coming to an end. Early in 1990 Elizabeth Clare Prophet made national headlines when she gathered together her New Age church—the Church Universal and Triumphant—in bomb shelters in anticipation of a nuclear attack in March or April 1990. Heeding her summons, 2,500 followers huddled in forty-five elaborately constructed bomb shelters in Montana's Paradise Valley, waiting for the end to come. After a couple of months her church was once again in the news when residents and state officials complained that the church was polluting the area because the shelters had an inadequate sewer system.[16]

As I saw these reports on the news, I remembered the people I saw when I went to one of her seminars and I wondered what was going to happen to them. Would this be another repeat of the Jim Jones mass suicide, or would it be a passing phase that would cause her followers to turn away from her? As I thought about this I realized that if I had embraced her teachings, I could have been one of those people gathered in fear under the earth hoping to escape the ravages of the nuclear attack she had said was sure to come at any minute.

In *Century's End* Hillel Schwartz tells of the mindset people have as they wait for the world to end at the close of the century.

> As usual we come to our end of century as others have come to theirs—convinced of exhaustion, extreme peril, exorbitant risk, explosive transformation. This *fin de siècle*, like those before it, is the last gasp, the critical moment, the overture to a new age. Everything we love is falling apart around us and we can only hope for a good death; everything we deplore is falling away and the pangs of a great birth are upon us. At century's end we are inevitably host to an oxymoronic time: the best and the worst, the most desperate and the most exultant; the most constrained and the most chaotic.[17]

This millennial fervor is especially hot this time around because we come to the end of 2,000 years of history, two millennia, and the beginning of a third. At the end of the first millennium, millennial fervor rose to its own heights of excess and expectation when people throughout Europe expected the end of the world on January 1, 1000.

On the eve of the millennium, people gathered in cathedrals across Europe. Some of the rich had sold their land and had given their money to the poor in the hope of obtaining salvation in the afterlife that was soon to follow. But the fateful hour passed without consequence: The world did not end. Church bells rang out, enemies embraced, and the world was reborn anew.[18]

The difference between the first millennium of the year 1000 and the second one coming in the year 2000 is that apocalyptic fears are not based solely on religious or spiritual foundations. This time around, the world as a whole faces some very serious problems about which boomers are becoming increasingly alarmed, chief among them being a concern for the environment.

The stark consequences of the Gulf War and of the Chernobyl nuclear accident are driving home the point that the world is at risk. Few of us can erase from our minds the images of oil wells boiling over with flames as they spewed tons of poisonous gas into the air during the war. When the fighting was over, more than 600 wells were found to be on fire. These fires were burning an estimated 6 million barrels of oil a day worth $100 million, three times the amount of Kuwait's prewar daily total.[19] Add to this the Gulf oil spill and the effects of the destruction of chemical and nuclear weapons facilities, and you end up with an environmentalist's worst nightmare. Even more telling, Iraqi casualties were estimated by some to be as high as 200,000 people during the six weeks of war.

While much of the damage to Kuwait and the Gulf was in the open, the effects of Chernobyl have proven to be silent and deadly. On April 29, 1986, a planned shutdown of the nuclear power plant's Number 4 reactor caused a thermal explosion that released a radioactive cloud, contaminating most of Europe. The main contamination took place in an eighty-mile circle and still affects over 2.2 million people. Of those affected, 400,000 are children who are the most susceptible to developing some form of cancer as a result of being exposed to the worst industrial accident ever known. The estimated cost to the former Soviet Union and to the people of the Ukraine is $360 billion and countless lives disrupted, uprooted, or lost.[20] Equally frightening are the Chernobyl-like reactors still in use which are accidents waiting to happen.

At the time of the explosion, Olga Korbut, who won three gold medals at the 1972 Olympic Games, lived in Minsk, 180 miles from Chernobyl. Part of the region is still heavily contaminated. In a *Time* article, "Who Knows How Many Will Die?", she told reporters that children in her town were shown plastic models of birds and trees because they were not allowed to go into the woods to see the real thing.[21] All of us must face some tough questions: What's in store for the children of the future? Will the world wake up in time?

As Earth Day 1990 approached, numerous reports were distributed concerning the state of the earth. Headlines such as "Planet Worse Off Since First Earth Day in 1970"[22], "4.6 billion pounds of toxic chemicals released in 1988,"[23] and "Vanishing Forest Fells Way of Life"[24] highlighted the growing concerns over the environment. Maura Dolan and Larry B. Stammer, environmental writers for the *Los Angeles Times*, reported that in contrast to the '70s, today the world is facing the loss of its tropical forests, the extinction of half its species, and the danger of the greenhouse effect, which would cause widespread climatic change and damage throughout the earth.[25]

These environmental concerns hit home when my house was sprayed with the pesticide malathion during the spring of 1990 in an attempt to eradicate the Medfly in the Los Angeles basin. In an eerie sight reminiscent of a scene from the Vietnam movie *Apocalypse Now*, five helicopters, flying in formation in the middle of the night, doused my yard as they flew over my neighborhood. As their blades thundered over my roof, I wondered if the malathion would do more than simply attack Medflies. I wondered what it would do to me. If dogs had to be brought into the house, and if fish ponds had to be covered, what did that say about the chemical's effects on my health and the health of my family?

Oftentimes we do not make the connection between our consumption and the environment. In 1981 during the height of the Cabbage Patch doll craze, I was in Hong Kong visiting my wife's friends. On a tour of the city, they proudly showed me the factory where the Cabbage Patch dolls were made. The factory was beside a waterway that ran into the ocean. I could see a pipe sprouting from the edge of the factory. The pipe was dumping a bluish-green mixture of what must have been untreated pollutants directly into the water. I did not say anything about it, but in the back of my mind some questions gnawed at me.

In our mania for trendsetting products, what are we doing to people in the Third World who do not have the environmental protection agencies that we have in the United States? In our pursuit of consumer goods made of plastics and chemicals, what are we doing to ourselves and the generations that will follow us?

Events such as the oil spills in Alaska and in the Persian Gulf, the nuclear fallout from Chernobyl, and oil fires in Kuwait make it clear that our well-being as humans is tied to our relationship with the earth. Consider the following statements.

• The world population is expected to double in the next 100 years,

and 90 percent of that growth will occur in poorer developing nations.[26]
- Earthquakes on the West Coast are impending.
- Air pollution is increasing.
- Higher levels of toxic wastes are found in water supplies.
- Acid rain is falling.
- There's a hole in the ozone layer.
- Forty thousand children in poor nations die from starvation every day.
- The world has a growing number of environmental refugees (10 million, projected to 50 million by 2050).[27]
- We don't know what to do with trash and where to store nuclear wastes.

These add up to what seem to be insurmountable problems which will be inherited by the baby boom generation and their children in the coming years.

Lester R. Brown of Worldwatch points out the drastic changes people will have to make if the environment is going to be preserved and protected for the future. Phasing out fossil fuels, stopping the deforestation of the earth, and putting a hold on population growth are just a few of the major ecological challenges faced by our generation.

The generation that is going to have to make these necessary changes to save the environment is the baby boomer generation. The motivation for this change has to be more than economic or political: It has to come deep from the soul as a response to one's understanding of the sacredness of the earth. Jan Hartke, religious liaison for Earth Day '90, challenged Amercia's faith communities to wake up to the need to add a spiritual dimension to the environmental battle that the corporate, scientific, and political communities have already begun to wage.[28]

U.S. Environmental Protection Agency chief, William K. Reily, told a group of Catholic leaders that because the natural world has an intrinsic spiritual value, a new vision of conservation grounded in religious faith could be a powerful force for change.[29]

Unfortunately, beyond the environment other problems abound. Drug use and gang wars plague the inner cities. Crimes associated with drugs and gangs have become such widespread problems that the number of persons in federal and state prisons doubled from 330,000 in 1980 to 670,000 in 1989. Using crime data from the U.S. Justice Department, the Sentencing Project reported in February 1990 that one of four black men in his twenties is under the control of the criminal justice system, whether in jail, on probation, or in court. This means that young baby boom blacks are becoming an endangered species.[30] Another report said that the firearm death rate for black teen males was 2.8 times the rate for natural causes in 1988 and that the firearm death rate for all teens ages 15 to 19 rose 43 percent from 1984 to 1988.[31]

Increasingly, the gang culture is moving from the big city to small towns and is not limited to ethnic minorities. In Colorado Springs, a city without housing projects, ghettos, or barrios, authorities in 1990 began noticing white youths among the followers of gang members who had arrived from Los Angeles. Jake Garcia, a school disciplinary officer in this city of 215,000, points out that the issue is not ethnicity. The problem has to do with kids who are left alone to do their own things, kids from single-parent families, kids who are hurting—all of whom need to belong to something or someone. Garcia commented that no community is immune from this: The whole country is ripe.[32]

Along with crime and drugs are additional problems: the U.S. education system, which has been said to trail other industrial nations in quality and effectiveness; the growing AIDS epidemic; the destabilization of the health care industry; the budget deficit; the clean-up of the savings and loans institutions; and the projections of the failure of the Social Security system when boomers retire. Mortimer B. Zuckerman, editor-in-chief of *U.S. News & World Report*, said in February 1990:

> America is happy to have won the cold war. But while we cheer, we are busy losing the hot war for America's economic future. Behind the false glitter of the prosperity of the 1980's, America is suffering grievous economic damage. Our saving and net investment are declining, our national and foreign debt is soaring and our real interest rates are rising to record levels. The inflation-adjusted wages of American labor are falling and have been falling for 15 years. Our infrastructure is crumbling, our educational system is deteriorating and our reputation for quality manufacturing and our leadership in technology are being squandered. Our sovereign control over our finances, our money supply and our interest rates is weakening, and our foreign markets are declining in industry after industry. There is still an American dream. This is not it.[33]

As exciting as the Gulf War was, it proved to be a brief respite between the growing problems faced by the average American. Dr. D. Ray Bardill, dean of the School of Social Work at Florida State University and president of the American Association of Marriage and Family Therapy, said that the Gulf War was in many ways a distraction from the real problems people face on an everyday basis. Like the hype of Super Bowl Sunday, Americans had to face Monday on the day after the war. This left many people with an empty, lost feeling.[34]

The discerning reader by this point will probably want to take the advice of one of the most popular bumper stickers of the '60s—"America, Love It or Leave It"—and take the next boat out, travel to a foreign land, and settle in a tropical paradise. Given these sets of conditions, is it any wonder that millennialism will catch fervor as the year 2000 approaches?

Will the year 2000 be a repeat of the year 1000? Is the year 2000 just another year on the calendar, or is it something more? For baby boomers this is a key question because when they reach the height of their leadership and economic power during their forties and fifties in the year 2000, their decisions about the future will greatly affect their standard of living and their spiritual values as they move into the twenty-first century.

Many Americans have already put on the sackcloth and ashes and have begun to wail in the streets about our upcoming doom. Others have decided to try to do something about it. Businesses have taken notice of a newfound "green" movement among former yuppies who have decided to buy products that are environmentally safe. Other boomers are volunteering in a host of charitable organizations to help the homeless, to try to prevent and cure AIDS, and to fight against drug abuse.

Still many people point to America's seeming collapse as a sign that Judgment Day is around the corner. Who is to say that they are not right? After all, even Jesus said, "About that day or hour no one knows, neither the angels in heaven, nor the Son, but only the Father. Beware, keep alert; for you do not know when the time will come" (Mark 13:32-33).

The challenge for the baby boom generation is to determine the kind of future it wants for itself, the Apocalyptic disaster or the dream of a new millennium of freedom, equality, and peace. The problem for the baby boom generation is that in order to save the world, it is going to have to work with the world. If it wants to save the planet, this generation is going to have to do something that is very hard to do: It will have to sacrifice its own needs and wants on behalf of others.

The irony for baby boomers is that while their parents went from a depression to an age of abundance, baby boomers are going to have to back off from the materialistic expectations abundance has produced in order to have a future for their children that is worth living. John Lennon's haunting song *Imagine* talks about a world in which there is no heaven or hell, no countries or religion, no possessions or greed. Although many would say this is impossible and many would say this is undesirable, Lennon's words convey a simple truth: In sharing the world instead of trying to conquer it, in giving instead of taking, we can live with the world as one.

Chapter Nine

GLOBALISM

A walk down the street where I live reveals a lot about the changing face of America. I live in a housing tract built in 1987 on the outskirts of Los Angeles. My neighbors are all baby boomers, and five of the families in our cul-de-sac have had babies in the last year. The jobs we have are varied: two police officers, two accountants, two dentists, three secretaries, a waitress, a manager of a golf course, a tow-truck operator, an engineer, an insurance executive, and two homemakers. This neighborhood, which sounds much like the one I grew up in, is different in one respect—it is global.

The ethnic make-up is one that would be found in few places in the world outside of the United States. The family next door to me is African-American. Next to them is a Hispanic-American family. The next one down is Euro-American. On the corner is a family from Morocco. Going up the other side of the street is another Hispanic family, two Euro-American families, and a family in which the husband is Chinese-American and the wife is Japanese-American. On the other side of me is a family comprised of a husband who is Filipino-American and a wife who is Euro-American. Next to them is a family with a Euro-American husband and a Hispanic-American wife. Last there is my family. I am a Euro-American mixture of Swedish, Norwegian, German, and English; my wife is Chinese-American; and my daughter is Eurasian-American.

This unusual mixture of ethnic groups and countries of origin is the wave of the future for all of America. In a May 1989 report from *American Demographics*, Joe Schwartz and Thomas Exter said that by the year 2010, 38 percent of Americans under the age of eighteen will belong to minority groups. This increase in minorities will be seen especially in particular states in the U.S.

By 2010, 80 percent of children in Hawaii will be nonwhite or Hispanic. "Minorities" will also form the majority of children in New Mexico (77 percent), California (57 percent), Texas (57 percent), New York (53 percent), Florida (53 percent), and Louisiana (50 percent). In the District of Columbia, 93 percent of children will be minorities by 2010.[1]

These kinds of percentages are already found in Glendale, California, a once conservative, Euro-American, middle-class city, which has changed dramatically in the last ten years. A 1990 study done by the school district found that 63 percent of the children spoke a primary language other than English. Surprisingly, Armenian had become the most common foreign language, boosting it above Spanish, Korean, and Filipino/Tagalog. In some schools, such as Mann Elementary, 91 percent of the students had a primary language other than English.

Needless to say, the challenges for teachers are great. According to the report, a newly enrolled student with little or no English needs about three years of special English tutoring and services before he or she can be fully integrated into a school's English-speaking environment. Sally Buckley, a school principal and an education specialist for the Glendale schools, feels good about the success they have had in helping students achieve proficiency in English. In the 1989 school year 1,014 students were reclassified as fluent in English.[2]

In Orange County, California, known as the bastion of Euro-American power and politics, the 1990 census showed that 48 percent of the student population were minorities, with the largest increases coming in the Latino and Asian populations.[3] This pattern holds true for the United States as a whole. From 1980 to 1990 Asians increased their numbers by 107 percent and Hispanics by 53 percent. Perhaps the most significant number coming out of the census is that 1 out of 4 Americans is a "minority."[4]

It is no mistake that the strongest, most populous, and most influential states of the next century—California, New York, Florida, and Texas—are in the list of states which will have the highest percentage of minorities. The economic and cultural boom that is taking place in these states is tied to the melding of the North American–born population with new immigrants who form a unique synthesis of culture combined with technological and economic innovation. The results of this will make an impact on all areas of our society, especially work, education, and religion. Those who approach these changes with the values of globalism will help to usher in a new future. As Schwartz and Exter say,

Over the next 20 years, children will lead the way toward an even more diverse future. . . . The states and local areas most blessed with children will be challenged by a profusion of races and cultures. Our children may show us the future even before they become adults.[5]

The nature and form of this future will be shaped by the way the baby boom generation accepts the challenges that it will bring. The events of 1989 through 1991 showed us how fast things could change. From Tiananmen Square, to the fall of the Berlin Wall, to the Romanian Revolution, to the downfall of communism in Eastern Europe, to the events surrounding the Gulf War, to the Russian Revolution, we were moved, frightened, exhilarated, and shaken by the accounts and images of a world undergoing revolution.

There are two things that are important in what we saw. First, the world as we knew it, with the Soviet Union at one end of the spectrum opposed by the United States at the other, was no longer viable. A new world order would be emerging in the 1990s. America would now have to take a fresh look at the world and would have to form its international relations with these new realities in mind.

Second, what we saw we took for granted. The fact that we could sit in our homes and witness many of these events firsthand was an outstanding miracle in itself. The technology that was required is a sign that the species we call human has taken a leap forward on the evolutionary scale. This dramatic change was ushered in by the development of the first computer, the ENIAC, which came on stream in 1946, which incidentally was the first year of the baby boom. Peter Drucker puts it succinctly: "In 1946, with the advent of the computer, information became the organizing principle of production. With this, a new basic civilization came into being."[6]

The management of information as the organizing principle for production is a shift from the past. Since the birth of the United States in 1776, the world has seen four surges of entrepreneurship that have changed the way people live. The first was the "Commercial Revolution," which followed the development of the first ocean-going freighter capable of carrying heavy payloads over large distances. This allowed an explosion of trade to take place between countries that had been separated by oceans.

The second entrepreneurial surge, which began in the middle of the eighteenth century and lasted into the middle of the nineteenth century, was the "Industrial Revolution." It ushered in an age of technology that shaped the world with the production of machinery, enabling humans to organize themselves into blocks of production. Social institutions, such as the modern army, the civil service, the Post Office, and the commercial bank, all owe their creation to the forces of the Industrial Revolution.

The third entrepreneurial surge began in 1870 with the invention of original products. Not only had they never been made before, but they quickly became accessible in large quantities: electricity, the telephone, electronics, steel, chemicals, pharmaceuticals, automobiles, and airplanes.

We are now in the fourth surge, triggered by information and biology.[7] In the Industrial Age technology was controlled by large organizations. The totalitarian state stood as the ultimate creation of the Industrial Age because power rested in the ability to control the populace through a centralized government run by a cadre of elite leaders. The effectiveness of the totalitarian state depended on three things: the cooperation of the people, the plans of the centralized government, and the control of information.

The breakdown of the Eastern Bloc is directly related to the fruition of the Information Age. With the advance of information-based technology, the totalitarian state is no longer able to control its people's access to knowledge. Computers, fax machines, satellite dishes, VCRs, telephones, televisions, and radios break down the borders between countries. As technology becomes more personalized, the totalitarian state loses its ability to keep people on the course of the "Big Lie": that state heads know what is best for the people, that they have all the answers, that they have the correct ideology, and that they can provide for all the needs of the people. In a sign of the times, one of the first laws abolished in the new Romania was the one that had outlawed typewriters during the Ceausescu regime.

In the Industrial Age technology served the interests of big government and big business by providing them with the means of control and production. In the Information Age technology serves the interests of the individual, freeing persons to make their own decisions as to what is best for them.

The laborer is now replaced by the knowledge worker—the specialist, the expert, the professional, and the technician. Unlike laborers who are tied to a particular position in the manufacturing process of a particular industry, such as a steam fitter in construction work, knowledge workers are mobile and flexible in their career options. For example, an accountant can work for a construction company as well as for a hospital, a retail business, a government agency, a gasoline station, or a car manufacturer. He or she is limited only by skill and willingness to relocate.

The power of knowledge workers rests in the knowledge they possess in their area of expertise. In their field they have more knowledge than their employer. In an accounting business, the computer programmer who designs the program for the new tax season is much more important than an individual accountant. The accountant can be replaced much more easily than the person who designed the software. If the computer goes down, everyone, including the owner of the company, is at the mercy of the ability of the computer programmer. Until the computer is up and running, no one works. As a result, rather than being under the control of the boss, the knowledge worker is superior to the employer in the worker's field of expertise. So, no matter where he or she may stand on the organizational hierarchy, the knowledge worker is an associate and a colleague.

Key to the knowledge workers' marketability is their continuing education, which keeps them abreast of the lastest changes, and the fact that almost every business needs people who are versed in computers, accounting, marketing, personnel management, word processing, and so on. This means that instead of being tied to one company, knowledge workers are free to move and to choose at will. They have the flexibility that a laborer could never have. The worker in a steel mill is tied to the success and failure of the company and the industry in a way that no industrial engineer would ever be. If the steel mill closes, the engineer can move to a different company in a different town, whereas the steel worker is unemployable until he or she gets retrained for another job.

Churches that have tried to minister to baby boomers often find it difficult to meet their needs because boomers have so many options. If they do not like a particular church, they seem to be all too willing to try another one. C. Peter Wagner says:

> Baby Boomers' sense of loyalty and commitment is very much lower than the preceding generation. So that those in my generation, if they ever started buying Chevy cars, that would be the only kind we would think of buying because there is a sort of a brand loyalty. If we bought Shell gasoline, we would never buy another kind. Even if it cost more, we would buy it. You don't find that in Baby Boomers. We live in an age where there are multiple choices of everything in life. Our whole life is thirty-one flavors. What Baby Boomers are saying is organized religion as they have known it is not what they are looking for. The denominational loyalty is low; this is true even in local church affiliation. As long as the "me" generation is not satisfied, they will keep looking until they are."[8]

This church-hopping has denominational leaders worried. Boomers are not retained because of denominational labels such as "United Methodist" or "Southern Baptist." They stay because a particular church has made them feel at home and meets their individual needs.

When baby boomers switch churches or try another faith, they are simply doing what they have been taught to do since they were born. Twenty to thirty to forty years of being bombarded with commercials have turned boomers into smart shoppers who can spot the flaws and the fakes rather easily. Rather than be shocked that a baby boomer would go to a channeler or look for meaning in a New Age book written by Shirley MacLaine, we should be surprised that they have not already tried it.

Churches that approach boomers with the naive assumption that they are the only ones who offer "the truth" fail to realize that boomers exhibit the characteristics of the knowledge worker when it comes to personal faith. They actively look for many different truths in a wide variety of places. Much of the popularity of Joseph Campbell's *The Power of Myth*, which became a best-seller and as a PBS series scored the highest ratings the network had seen, can be attributed to boomers' pursuit of knowledge in the spiritual arena.

The Power of Myth is a conversation between journalist Bill Moyers and the late Joseph Campbell, who taught for almost forty years at Sarah Lawrence College on the subject of myth. In one part of their conversation, they talk about the difference between myth and theology.

MOYERS: Religion begins with the sense of wonder and awe and the attempt to tell stories that will connect us to God. Then it becomes a set of theological works in which everything is reduced to a code, to a creed.

CAMPBELL: That's the reduction of mythology to theology. Mythology is very fluid. Most of the myths are self-contradictory. You may even find four or five myths in a given culture, all giving different versions of the same mystery. Then theology comes along and says it has got to be just this way. Mythology is poetry, and the poetic language is very flexible.

Religion turns poetry into prose. God is literally up there, and this is literally what he thinks, and this is the way you've got to behave to get into proper relationship with that god up there.

Moyers points out that we don't have to believe there was a historic King Arthur in order to "get" the stories around him. But we have to believe there was a Christ; otherwise, miracles just don't make sense.[9]

This conversation brings to the surface what people find to be important in the area of personal faith. Rather than looking for a theology or a religion with a set of literal truths and creeds, boomers are looking for what speaks to their hearts. Campbell appealed to baby boomers because his spirituality was not focused on rites and creeds. Instead he found truths in the stories of heroism, love, sacrifice, and bliss found around the globe. Campbell captured the imagination by revealing the meaning of these stories to modern civilization. He says that today's world is "demythologized." The result is that people are interested in mythology because "myths bring them messages. . . . They're stories about the wisdom of life."[10]

The globalization of culture means that the individual has equal access to the beliefs, myths, and stories of cultures from around the world. The source of these stories is the mass media, which link our planet together. Before the invention and the dissemination of television, the printed word carried with it an authority of its own, passed down through the ages from one generation to the next. The most cherished object in the home for many early Americans was the Bible. Not only was it a source book for faith, it was also the tool for education and for learning.

I discovered this in the first church where I served as pastor. I often visited Neil Brown, a diminutive lady of my congregation who was one year short of her one hundredth birthday. One day as I was reading a psalm to her, I noticed that she was saying the words right along with me. I went to the next psalm and noticed she did the same thing. I asked her about it and she told me when she was a little girl she memorized the psalms; it was part of her education and religious training.

Today it is almost illegal to read the psalms in school, and it certainly would not be at the heart of an educational curriculum. In fact, baby boomers and their children may not even be sure what a psalm is, let alone be able to recite one from memory. Whereas a preacher in Neil Brown's day could make an allusion to a biblical figure to make a point in a sermon because everyone would understand what was being referred to, those ministering to this generation can make no such assumption.

The authority for Neil Brown's generation was the Bible, the Word of God, whose stories and accounts formed a common culture upon which the rules and standards of society were built. Authority in the 1990s is found in the mass media—in the pages of a newspaper or in flickering images of modern icons found on television. Ted Koppel has far more credibility to people than the most adroit preacher. The thirty-second commercial propels political candidates into office far more effectively than any book every could.

Today the word is processed, not written. Truth is conveyed through sight and sound mixed together in complex formulas at the cost of millions of dollars to convey the message of "the sponsor." Thomas H. Troeger, professor of preaching at Colgate-Rochester Divinity

School, Crozer Theological Seminary, says that to reach this generation, preachers must practice "imaginative theology." "Imaginative
theology employs the visionary and integrative capacities of the mind
to create theological understanding. It uses the powers of observation
to become receptive to the Holy Spirit, who works upon our consciousness through patterns of association and juxtaposition."[11] Instead of
fighting the images of the mass media, pastors need to be "paying
attention to the mass media images that are shaping people's imaginative worlds."

Whereas in the past they tried to harmonize the authorities of science and the Bible, today's pastors find that, for the people they are
trying to reach, "the authority of Scripture has become as questionable
as the authority of modern science and technology. . . . Appeals to the
Bible or tradition do not carry sufficient weight in themselves."[12]

> Before we can preach those sacred visions effectively, we need to
> understand how our listeners imagine the world. They do not live in
> biblical times or reformation times or even modern times. They live
> in the postmodern, mass media age that has conditioned them to
> perceive and experience the world in new ways."[13]

One of the new ways people experience the world is through technology, which conditions them to the need for information. Information—about the rise and fall of the stock exchange, the value of the
dollar in Japan, the number of components it takes to build a computer,
and the results of the latest poll—is what makes the postmodern world
go around.

Information shows have proliferated on television. CNN broadcasts
news twenty-four hours a day. Other networks offer documentaries and
half-hour information shows such as *Entertainment Tonight*, which
narrows its focus on one segment of society, the entertainment world.
Nightline, one of the first of these information-based programs, has
great influence because of the breadth of its subject matter. Bringing
into the home the international leaders of the world, it uses the most
advanced technology to keep people abreast of the latest issues and
stories on a worldwide basis.

Because so much faith is placed in information, people are at the
mercy of the technology that brings the information to them. Rather
than shortening the work week or making our lives simpler, the technology of the Information Age has caused people to work harder to
keep up with the latest advances and has forced them to keep retrain-
ing themselves in seminars and classes in order to keep a job.

As a result, society is losing perspective on the human sense of time.

Computerization means that everyone expects everything to work faster. Instead of conversing with a checkout clerk at a store, we impatiently wait for our groceries to be scanned by a computer. Restaurant managers promise your food in ten minutes, or they will pay the bill. Telephone calls are greeted by disembodied voices on machines, which tell us to push a series of buttons to reach the person we want. All of these measures are attempts to speed the process.

Philip T. Nicholson, a Boston medical writer, is concerned because someone needs to be thinking about the glue that will hold people together. Because of the proliferation of the communications revolution, people are undergoing "technostress"; they cannot handle all the information that is at their disposal.[14]

In the same article, Craig Brod, a Silicon Valley psychotherapist, is troubled because we seem to be creating a society that does not understand human values. He even has patients who ask him how much time they should spend with their kids. In many ways he sees us automating the human element from our lives.[15]

By taking these things into consideration, the savvy communicator of the faith will not deluge listeners with more information or appeal to traditional authorities to make a case. Instead the communicator will bring to mind images and stories about the human element to which people can relate. Rather than present readymade answers, the speaker explores the questions and brings the truth to light in an experience of wonder and awe. In a world that is used to the dramatic form of communication, communicators must use poetry, not prose, must sing, not speak, and must reveal, not tell, if they have any hope at all of reaching this generation.

Globalization not only affects the individual and his or her choices; it affects the society as a whole. In the business world the economy has become transnational; it is not bound by the limits of nationalism and provincialism. Whereas in the '50s the United States dominated the world market, in the '90s it meets stiff competition as it battles to keep its share of the market.

Today, economics is international and transnational. It transcends the nation state and is focused instead on markets. In the Industrial Age the nation state wielded the most power and had the most control over its economic future. In the Information Age the transnational economy has four such units of power. Peter Drucker states:

The nation state is one of these units; individual countries—especially the major, developed, non-Communist ones—matter, of course. But increasingly decision-making power is shifting to a second unit, the region—the European Economic Community; North America; tomorrow perhaps a Far Eastern region grouped around Japan. Third, there is a genuine and almost autonomous world economy of money, credit, and investment flows. It is organized by information that no longer knows national boundaries. Finally, there is the transnational enterprise—not necessarily a big business, by the way—which views the entire developed non-Communist world as one market, indeed, as one "location," both to produce and to sell goods and services.[16]

The result of the transnational economy is that there are no more superpowers. The reason is that the goal of economics has changed from maximizing profits to maximizing markets. Instead of focusing on the amount of money made, companies are more concerned with market share.

We have been quite familiar with this concept in the television industry. Each week the ratings come out to reveal which show has been the most popular during the week and which did the best in its particular time spot. The cost charged to advertisers for sponsoring a program is based on the ratings a television program receives. During the course of a year the viewing public goes through "sweeps-weeks" when ratings are taken to determine these fees. The networks show their best programs during those times. Local television news programs bring out the juiciest stories, the networks show special movies and mini-series, weekly television series spice up their shows, and no one airs reruns.

The goal of each program is to increase its market share so that it has the highest number of viewers in its time spot, thus giving it the highest rating. A super-hit show, such as *The Cosby Show* during the late 1980s, wipes out the competition during its time spot and virtually ensures that any show that is shown at the same time on any other channel will get dismal ratings and eventually will be canceled.

In the transnational economy the same has become true for products, only the ratings are determined by how many units are bought and the field of play is the world. It is not enough to do well in the United States or in England. To truly succeed and stay in business, today's companies compete for market share worldwide. Central to the ability to compete is the ability to produce products in a given region.

Americans have been somewhat surprised by the willingness of the Japanese to build cars in the United States. Major Japanese auto companies now manufacture their cars in the United States, and some even ship the completed product back to Japan. The reason for this is twofold: first, to increase production; and, second, to be close to the American market, to understand what will appeal to the American customer. Drucker says: "Investment used to follow trade. Now trade follows investment. Proximity to, and 'feel' for, the market becomes decisive. And that requires a base within the market; it requires market presence and market standing. It requires investment in production, in other words."[17]

The rise of Japan in the world marketplace brings to our attention another vital point in understanding the transnational economy: The world is no longer centered around Europe; the future belongs to the Pacific Rim. The Pacific Rim includes all the peoples touched by the Pacific Ocean. This extensive area stretches from the west coast of South America northward, across the Bering Strait to the Russian Federation, and south down the Asian continent to Australia.

The main ingredient in its rise is demographic. In 1990 Asia had half the world's population. By the year 2000 it will have two-thirds, while Europe will only have 6 percent. In landmass, Asia's Pacific Rim region is twice as large as Europe and the United States. Even more astounding is its economic growth and potential. In 1990 the Pacific Rim was a $3 trillion market, growing at a rate of $3 billion a week.[18] In *Megatrends 2000* John Naisbitt emphasizes the following points:

1. The Pacific Rim shift is economically driven—and at a pace that is without precedent.
2. The shift is not only economic but cultural as well. The countries of the Pacific Rim speak more than 1,000 languages and have the most varied religious and cultural traditions in the world.
3. Although Japan is the region's economic leader today, the East Asia region (China and the Four Tigers—South Korea, Taiwan, Hong Kong, and Singapore) will eventually dominate.
4. The Pacific Rim's economic thrust is being reinforced with a commitment to education. As early as 1985, a higher percentage of young Koreans attended schools of higher education than young Britons.[19]

Other facts and figures should be considered when contemplating the future of the Pacific Rim. Increased population does not always portend disaster. As the Pacific Rim increases, the living standards of its population will become more consumer based than survivor based. By 2000 Japan and the Four Tigers will have 13 million net new consumers. In the next wave of developing countries—Thailand, Malaysia, Indonesia, and the Philippines—there will be an additional 68 million. This is not even counting China which could have 100 million new customers with disposable income depending on political and economic reforms. In comparison, Europe will have only an additional 11 million net new customers by the year 2000.[20]

The rise of the Pacific Rim does not necessarily portend the decline of the United States as much as it announces the end of European rule in colonies around the world. In 1997 when Great Britain gives Hong Kong back to China and in 1999 when Portugal gives Macau back to China, it will signal the end of the European colonial system which was able to control the economy of the world and to keep its subject people under its power for over 500 years.

The same holds true for the European dominance of Christianity. In 1492 when Columbus discovered the Americas for Europe, 93 percent of the world's Christians were European. Christian theology, music, worship, and arts were built on a European culture and lifestyle. But by the year 2000 only 21 percent of the world's Christians will live in Europe. This statistic represents both a blessing and a challenge to Christians around the globe. The goal of Christianity has always been to spread the gospel to people around the world. Now that these efforts have borne fruit, the question faced by Christians is, Where do we go from here?

A snapshot of world Christianity shows us the following:

PERCENTAGE OF CHRISTIANS WORLDWIDE

	1980	1991	2000
EUROPE	31%	25%	21%
RUSSIAN REPUBLICS	7%	7%	6%
NORTH AMERICA	14%	11%	10%
AFRICA	12%	15%	17%
EAST ASIA	1%	5%	7%
SOUTH ASIA	8%	9%	10%
LATIN AMERICA	26%	27%	29%
OCEANIA	1%	1%	1%[21]

While the total number of Christians has grown in all categories (for example, Europe will grow from 403 million to 411 million between 1980 and 2000), the most rapid growth is taking place in Africa whose numbers will grow from 164 million to 324 million, and in East Asia whose numbers are exploding from 16 million to 128 million from 1980 to 2000.[22]

Beyond raw numbers, The Economist, in a December 24, 1988, article on "New Christendom," tells how Western Europe has seen a decline in Christianity since World War II. The article tells how one in ten Western Europeans attends services on Sundays compared to one in three in 1850. Europe's loss of influence is most clearly seen in those who are willing to be leaders. For example, in the diocese of Santiago de Compostela, in Catholic Spain, the number of priests has fallen from 1,200 in 1965 to 200 in 1988; more Jesuits are produced in India than in Europe; and in northwest Wales one Methodist pastor serves seventeen congregations.[23]

Western Europe has seen a decline in religious faith owing to a number of factors, including a loss in intellectual confidence, a question of why a good God would allow such atrocities as the Jewish Holocaust to take place, and the anticlerical stance of many who suffered when religion and the state went hand in hand as seen in Spain and England throughout their histories. In contrast, the rest of the world is seeing a religious revival. While an Islamic revival is sweeping through the Middle East and Northern Africa, Christianity is welling up in countries such as South Korea, Kenya, and Bolivia.[24]

One of the most influential Christian pastors in the 1980s was Paul Yonggi Cho, pastor of the Yoido Full Gospel Central Church in Seoul, Korea, which has over 50,000 cell groups and 500,000 members, making it the largest church in the world. His books and seminars have sparked the cell group movement in the United States, and his understanding of God comes from Asian-based theology. In his book, *The Fourth Dimension*, he talks about the importance of having a vision.

> This is the reason the Holy Spirit comes to cooperate with us—to create, by helping young men see visions, and old men to dream dreams. Through envisioning and dreaming dreams we can kick away the wall of limitations, and can stretch out to the universe. That is the reason God's Word says, "Where there is no vision the people perish." If you have no vision, you are not being creative; and if you stop being creative, then you are going to perish.
>
> Visions and dreams are the language of the fourth dimension, and the Holy Spirit communicates through them. Only through a vision and a dream can you visualize and dream bigger churches. You can visualize a new mission field; you can visualize the increase of your church. Through visualizing and dreaming you can incubate your future and hatch the results.[25]

Visualizing and dreaming are not the common words of Karl Barth or Reinhold Niebuhr, at least not used in this sense. Cho's story of faith—of God giving him a vision of a church seating 10,000 people, of selling his house to purchase land when he had no other money, of God telling him to use women to form the leadership for his cell groups (which was quite radical for the Korean culture), of building the church with small cell groups—is a challenge to a European-based theology which tends to focus on theological speculation and intellectual ruminations about the demise of the faith.

As these Christians from non-European countries become missionaries to the world, their new-found faith will have strong influence throughout the worldwide Christian community. Even in the United States the new missionaries are the ones who come from overseas to minister in America. To many Christians, their example of faith and action is an inspiration and a call to witness.

The challenge for Western Christians will be to capture the new spirit of Christianity and to offer a faith that moves beyond mere rationalism to include the spiritual and experiential dimensions of the faith. The Christian's outlook will have to be global and open to the faith experiences of those who come out of Asia, Latin America, Africa, and Eastern Europe. As in so many areas of life, developing this willingness to be open and to learn from other cultural groups will not be an easy task.

But even with the global growth of the Christian faith, the same percentage of the world's population will be Christian in the year 2000 as it was in 1900, 34 percent. The percentage will remain the same because of the sheer numbers of people in the world. In the 100 years since 1900, the world's population will have grown from 1,619,886,800 to 6,251,055,000 and the number of people who have never heard of Christianity at all will number 1,038,819,000.[26]

Even with its diminishing role in the world, Western Europe is not ready to throw in the towel. Its banding together in the European Economic Community in 1992 makes it much easier for Western Europe to be a factor in the world market. Individual regulations, specifications, exchange rates, and checks at borders, all of which have protected European countries from one another, are going to be gone, allowing the European entrepreneur much greater freedom to develop and market a product in a region that will include over 400 million people.

Coupled with the reunification of Germany, the end of communism in Eastern Europe, and the Russian Republics, and the liberation of the Baltic states, Europe stands at the door of a new epoch in its history. But as it heads into the next century, Europe faces great challenges. While Western Europe unites in a European Economic Community, Eastern Europe faces chaos and strife as it sorts out the results of its various revolutions. Old scores remain to be settled as countries define new boundaries and set up new governments. Refugees from the East will try the patience of the West. The devastating effects of communism on Eastern Europe's economic system will take a long time to repair. The stability of the cold war is now replaced by uncertain alliances and new quests for power as people fight for the freedom for which they have longed.

The upshot of all this is that the world that baby boomers inherit from their parents, as they take up places of leadership in the 1990s and in the next century, is radically different from the one into which they were born. The world in which we now live is global. Whether we are talking about culture or economics or religion or even the environment, whatever happens in one nation affects the whole world.

But the changes in Europe and the rise of the Pacific Rim have brought a curious reaction from North Americans. In some ways we act like we have lost it all. In spite of our military victory in the Gulf and the fall of communism, there is still a suspicion in the North American mind that we have lost something, that in some way we are on a downward cycle of power and influence that will make the United States a second-rate nation, that we have lost our soul.

Part of this is an unwillingness to see that the '50s were an aberration born out of the ruins of war. The idea that Japan and Germany should bear the marks of war forever is born more out of envy than fear. As a result "Japan bashing" has become quite fashionable as America feels a need to protect itself from the rest of the world.

The problem baby boomers face is that as a generation they are isolationist in their own country. The "Portrait of a Generation" survey done by *Rolling Stone* clearly makes the point that "this generation is isolationist—in a world that is increasingly interdependent."[27] The key to understanding this isolationist attitude is that it springs from the boomers' detachment from the United States they grew up in and from the disappointments of their youth. As *Rolling Stone* points out in relation to the '60s experience:

A generation found itself outside the system and indeed opposed to the official leadership, whether it was the grassroots rebellion for civil rights or the popular opposition to the war. Instead of building a creative structure for the energies of the members of the generation, this dynamic exhausted their energies in conflict with the government and with one another. It taught them that the structure itself was corrupt, that individuals must follow their own moral compass and that they could not expect much moral leadership from above.

The nation's framework, the sense of larger purpose and pos-

sibilities inherited from their parents' era, collapsed for this generation. It no longer seemed believable. And nothing has happened since
to restore it.

Perhaps this is the last tragedy from the war in Vietnam—the way
in which it has crippled the idealism of an entire generation.[28]

Many see this isolationism as a negative, but when put in its context
it is not as bad as it seems. To compete in the transnational economy
and in the Information Age, a break with the past way of doing things is
necessary. While boomers may be isolated against an America that has
allowed injustice in racial relations; an America that is geared to the
teeth; an America where the rich get richer and the poor get poorer;
and America where the homeless sleep in the street ten miles away
from Beverly Hills; an America that has polluted its waters, land, and
air; an America that has seen its share of corrupt politicians and
profiteering businesspeople, the boomers' isolation from these things
is America's greatest strength and hope for the future.

While this generation may be turned off by this America, it is tuned
in to the world. Among its members are those who have traveled to the
far reaches of the earth, those who have served in the Peace Corps,
those who have served on military bases across the world, those who
have started multinational businesses, those who sang "We Are the
World" and raised millions of dollars for hunger relief, and those who
have experimented with different religious and cultural expressions of
life.

Rather than wanting to impose their views on others, baby boomers
are more likely to be open to the values, beliefs, and methods of other
cultures. More than that of any other generation the outlook of
boomers is global. This generation sees the link between the destruction of tropical forests in the Amazon River basin and the environment
of the world. This generation is going green, buying products on the
basis of their environmental impact. Boomers are the ones who are
open to the spiritualism of the East. This generation wants to hear the
voices of women and minorities. This generation has broken the color
line through interracial marriages. As a result, the baby boom generation is poised to benefit the most from globalism, the ability to see the
world as a whole and to value the culture and perspectives of people
different from themselves.

The strength of America is that it is an immigrant nation. The
United States is one of the few global nations on this earth. While
many citizens may cry out against the immigration of people from
Asia and Latin America, this immigration is what fuels the economy,

brings in new ideas, and establishes ties to the rest of the world. While Japan may seem to be growing stronger, its nationalism tied to racial background and cultural oneness eventually will weaken its ability to compete. As James Fallows notes in *More Like Us*:

> The truth is that racism runs through nearly all of the world, usually much more strongly than in the United States . . . . One of the things that makes America most unusual is its assumption that race should not matter, that a society can be built of individuals with no particular historical or racial bond to link them together. This is a noble belief: it makes America better than most other societies.[29]

This belief is at the heart of globalism: What matters is not the race or history of the person but rather the potential of the individual to make a new and lasting contribution to society. Rather than erect boundaries between people because of culture or outward appearance, globalism embraces cultural differences to see how they can enhance all of society, while at the same time affirming the right of the individual to maintain his or her own course. The right to free speech, freedom of religion, freedom of assembly, and private property all give rise to the ability of the individual to learn from others while still maintaining personal dignity.

While America asserts the right of the individual, other countries are caught in a different mindset. Tied to historical values and traditions, their goal is to maintain the values of their ancestors or to recapture the glories of the past. One thing that makes the establishment of the European Economic Community such a grand experiment is that for it to succeed, countries with rich traditions and sometimes old animosities, such as France and England, will have to give up some of their uniqueness to make it work. As with a reunified Germany, about which all Europeans have well-founded fears, the success of this new venture will rest on the ability of people to trust each other and to appreciate one another's traditions.

Similar dynamics affect the global potential of the relation between the United States and Asia. Though some countries that felt the crush of Japan's armies in World War II may fear Japan's current economic boom, much of Asia is convinced that Japan has surpassed America in world economic leadership.

To the Asian countries it seems as though their struggles are tied to history and geography, conditions imposed by nature. Japan ended up on small rock mountains. Korea is divided in half. The British could not hold on to Hong Kong forever. The Kuomintang lost to the communists and had to flee to Taiwan. But in their eyes, America is different. As Fallows states:

> America's difficulties, however, look to the Asians like failures of character, evidence that we no longer deserve our place. . . . The Americans had their huge, rich continent, they ran the world after the war, they had every advantage, and look at what's become of them! Many Asians have concluded that American society no longer functions in such a way as to make America strong.[30]

Many have embraced the idea that in order to compete against the Japanese we need to become like them. In *Shadows of the Rising Sun,* Jared Taylor recounts a conversation with another American who marveled at how much Japan had wrought in so short a time. Taylor asked, "Do you think we need to learn how to be more like the Japanese?" "Hell, no," his friend replied. "We need to be more like us."[31]

Being more like us means accepting and reaffirming the abnormal values of globalism, which give people the freedom to seek their own avenues while they benefit from the differences that people bring to the greater society. Rather than try to mold everyone into one cultural perspective and into one belief system, America must see that its future lies in a willingness to be enhanced and challenged by the new immigrants in its midst and by its openness to ideas that come from beyond the mainstream of middle-class, Euro-American America.

Recently I was in a discussion with church leaders about how to enhance the ministry of our churches. During the discussion I stated as a goal the development of ethnic leaders. After the meeting a Euro-American baby boomer came up to me and asked me to clarify my statement. She asked, "What do you mean by 'development'?"

I replied, "It is not so much development as it is giving them an opportunity to teach us."

She said: "Good. Many times when I hear the term 'ethnic development' it seems as though whites want them to become like us, instead of our becoming like them. I have been working with our youth and with youth from the Korean church. Recently I went to a camp with both groups, and the Korean youth led the closing worship service. Our youth were taken aback when the Korean youth began the service by the washing of feet. It was a very spiritual experience. There is a lot we can learn from them."

When Martin Luther King, Jr. made his famous "I Have a Dream" speech on the steps of the nation's capital during the heat of the civil rights movement in August 1963, he challenged America to let freedom ring and to join hands—no matter what race or religion—so that all people could rejoice in their liberty.[32]

If the boomer generation can heed this challenge; if it can move from isolationalism to globalism; if it can wake up to the dreams that make America great; if it can look beyond itself and embrace the immigrant, the ethnic, the non-European and the values they bring; if it can look beyond the borders of nations to affirm the cultural diversity of the world; if it can cry out for justice, freedom, and equal rights for all of God's children; then the United States will have no need to fear the future. Instead, it can lead the way.

Chapter Ten

WHOLENESS

The single most important demographic fact of the 1990s took place on January 1, 1991: The oldest baby boomer turned forty-five. This event signaled the beginning of a profound change of consciousness that will take place in boomers as they move toward the next century. They are no longer the young and the restless; instead they will be middle-aged and heading for retirement. There is nothing like realizing that your life expectancy is thirty-three more years to focus your attention on what is important.

This new stage of life will bring with it some pluses. People who are ages forty-five to fifty-five reach their peak earnings and well-being. They make decisions about work and home life that will prepare them for their "golden years." They enjoy family life and settle into the lifestyle it has taken decades to develop. They reexamine their values and focus on what they want to teach the next generation.

This change will make a huge impact on our society. In an *American Demographics* article on "Targeting the Prime-Life Consumer," Jeff Ostroff points out that the forty-five and older population will grow by 18 million people from 1990 to 2000. There will be no increase in the numbers of those under forty-five. Those eighteen to thirty-four in age will decline in number, causing businesses to develop new products and services for older Americans rather than to depend on marketing to the young.[1]

On the other side of the equation, the youngest boomer turned twenty-seven in 1991 and will not turn forty-five until 2009. As younger boomers, who were born from 1953 through 1964, go through the '90s, they will be focused on children, creating a career, and surviving economically. Rather than reaching a peak in their lives, they will find this decade to be a struggle.

Their challenge will be to establish families, to buy a home, and to educate their children in a time of diminishing government revenues and less money for education, aid to the poor, health programs, and housing. As the government seems to be running out of money, it will be raising taxes to try to maintain existing programs. This will hit younger boomers the hardest, as they are still working to establish themselves at work and at home.

Young boomers' chief contribution to the lifestyle of the '90s will be their children who are what demographers call the "baby boomlet." As these children grow, younger boomers will be concerned with family values and creating a better life for their children than they experienced in the turbulent '60s and '70s.

As boomers reach these next stages of life, their greatest desire will be for wholeness. They will want to close the circle of faith, work, family, and leisure into a complete package that will enable them to make some sense out of their lives. "Having it all" will mean knowing why you are doing things and for whom you are doing them. It will not be enough just to make money, to own a house, or to have kids. Instead, value will need to be distributed in every part of life to give one a feeling of well-being about the kind of lifestyle one has chosen to live. This desire for wholeness will play itself out in at least seven trends.

Rediscovery of the Family

Babies are in. The picture of Demi Moore, nude and pregnant, on the cover of *Vanity Fair* is simply one reflection of the newest trend. Her mother's generation would have been shocked to display pregnancy in such a public way. But not Demi. She was saying for all who cared to listen, "Look at me, I'm going to be a mom." She wasn't the only one. Connie Chung made the news just because she was trying to get pregnant at the age of forty-four. On television, Murphy Brown, of the hit series by the same name, became pregnant at age forty-two and decided to have her child even though she was single. The creators of *The Mary Tyler Moore Show* were never so bold. Even Sam Malone of *Cheers*, the single playboy of all time, wanted to be a father and was looking for the woman to carry his child. So what is going on? The baby boom generation is rediscovering the family.

For the first time since 1964, over 4 million babies were born in the United States in 1989. This caps a trend that began in the mid-'80s when births jumped from 2,918,000 in 1984 to 3,716,000 in 1985.[2]

The desire for motherhood before time runs out has pushed many single women to decide to have children. From 1980 to 1988 the birthrate among unmarried Euro-American women age thirty to thirty-four increased 68 percent, and in those ages thirty-five to thirty-nine there was a 69 percent jump.[3] While 10 percent of births in 1988 were to Euro-American single boomers, 40 percent were to African-

American single boomers, and 24 percent to Hispanic-American single women. Baby busters, ages eighteen to twenty-four showed an even higher percentage of births to single women: 29 percent of Euro-American births, 73 percent of African-American births, and 29 percent of Hispanic-American births were to single women.[4]

The biological clock and medical technology have combined to allow women to seek a number of options for having children without a husband. Adoption and insemination are just two options women have available to them. Beyond self-sufficiency, failed marriages, or the unavailability of the right man, a woman's natural reproductive cycle reminds her of the need to be part of a family. If she cannot have a husband, often she still wants to have a child. Paula Van Ness, executive director of the National Community AIDS Partnership in Washington, gives us an indication of what is going on. At the age of thirty-nine she concluded that she could go through life without a man, but not without a child.[5]

The 1990 Monitor Survey, which has a long track record of surveying America's social trends, contains some surprising findings. Since 1987 the survey has asked working women whether a list of possible reasons would allow them to stop working. Those who said having enough money would be reason enough to stop working registered 35 percent in 1987, 33 percent in 1988, and 38 percent in 1989. But in 1990 it jumped to 56 percent. The main reason women were ready to leave work was because they wanted to be with their children.

Another significant question showed that for the first time in twenty years, the number of women who favor a career for women dropped below 50 percent. Instead, many see part-time work as an attractive arrangement for women with children. Susan Hayward, senior vice president of Yankelovich Clancy Shulman, points out that while these attitudes have not been put into action, they signal a major shift in women's feelings about home and work.

But it is not just women who want to have children and a family life. The poll also showed that the share of men who describe their job as a career dropped to 48 percent in 1990. Younger men were especially dissatisfied with their jobs, and men in general wanted more time to spend with their families.[6] This was echoed in a 1989 poll conducted by Robert Half International, which found that 45 percent of men surveyed said they would refuse a promotion rather than miss time at home. They also found that 74 percent of men would rather have a "daddy track" job than a "fast track" one.

James Levine, director of the "Fatherhood Project" at Back Street College of Education in New York City, believes this "father hunger" is present in a large number of baby boomer men who missed out on a relationship with their own fathers. These men want things to be different for their own children.[7] But Edward Zigler, a Yale psychologist, puts this in perspective when he states that as yet there is no "daddy track" in corporate America.[8] The corporation is very unforgiving to the man who does not give it his all.

Like their fathers before them, baby boomer men find themselves squeezed between work and home. Lost beneath the discussion of feminism and women's rights has been the discussion of what a man's role should be in postfeminist America. Are men to be stoic or sensitive, silent or assertive, aggressive or submissive, family man or corporate man? Thirty years of criticism, much of it justified, has them confused, angry, and seeking a definition of manhood that they can live with.

On one side there is the desire to be husbands and fathers, almost a nostalgia to go back to the way it used to be. The *Father Knows Best* model is one that gives a man a sense of importance as one who has wisdom and guidance to share with the whole family and as someone who is appreciated. On the other side is the tough "Arnold Schwarzenegger" model whose fitness and virility are never questioned and who is victorious over the most daunting challenges imaginable. Even male mannequins in store windows reflect this vision of muscular competence as the mannequin for the '90s stands 6'2" instead of 6' and has a 42" chest instead of its previous 40".[9]

The rediscovery of the family means that boomers, male and female, will continue to define their roles in the family, but will be most concerned about how to raise the kids. One of the big issues for boomers is daycare. Unlike their parents' generation where dad worked and mom stayed home with the children, this generation is at work, men and women alike. In fact, in February 1986, women workers became the majority of professional employees in the United States. Since the end of World War II, women in the work force have increased 200 percent. David Bloom, an associate professor of economics at Harvard University, believes that the increase in the number of women in the work force is the most important change ever in the labor market in America.[10]

As a result, since 1970 there has been a tremendous increase in the number of children in daycare. In 1970, 24 percent of mothers with children under age one worked outside the home. By 1987 that figure jumped to 51 percent. In 1970, 30 percent of mothers with children under the age of six worked outside the home, which increased to 57 percent in 1987. Not all children are in daycare centers. In fact only 14.7 percent of children who are in one type of daycare or another are in daycare centers. The rest are cared for by babysitters at home (29.7

percent), in another's home (41.3 percent), in a nursery or school (7.6 percent), or by their mother at work (6.7 percent).[11]

Besides the problem of finding adequate daycare, boomers also face feelings of guilt about leaving their children, which is exacerbated by researchers who are trying to determine the effects of daycare on children. In a special issue of *Time*, Pat Wingert and Barbara Kantrowitz wrote an article on "The Day Care Generation." They report the following:

> One set of researchers argues that babies who spend more than 20 hours a week in child care may grow up maladjusted. Other experts say the high turnover rate among poorly paid and understaffed child-care workers has created an unstable environment for youngsters who need dependability and consistency. And still others are worried about health issues—the wisdom of putting a lot of small children with limited immunities in such close quarters.[12]

To cope with child care, boomers need assistance from churches and other groups right now. Daycare, after-school care, parent training workshops, prenatal care, and parent support groups are programs and services that are in heavy demand. As the baby boomlet grows up, the focus will shift to providing youth and young adult programs to meet their needs.

Split-shift parenting is an example of a growing trend for married boomers with children who are trying to figure out how to make it all fit together. In 1985 only 46 percent of women and 42 percent of men in nonagricultural occupations worked a typical forty-hour, five-day-a-week job. Instead parents were taking turns watching the kids while the other parent worked. Furthermore, in the same year one out of every six working mothers with children under fourteen and one out of every five working fathers held an evening or night job or a rotating shift. The upshot of this is that split-shift parents are full-time workers and caregivers. Instead of having time together, they share the burden of raising the kids and operate more like single parents with two incomes.[13]

The old concept of weekends off falls apart for these families. There is never any time off because the parents are constantly taking turns working or caring for the children. Because of the growth of service jobs, which have evening and weekend hours, working parents struggle with a schedule that is almost unbearable. The idea of going to church on Sunday morning is almost laughable to these families. Sunday morning might be the only time they get to say hello to each other—if one of them is not working a 10:00 A.M. shift at the mall.

Churches that are having the most success reaching boomers offer

Sunday evening or Wednesday evening services, complete with child-care, church school, and a full worship program. The Vineyard churches and the congregations patterned after Chuck Smith's Calvary Church in Costa Mesa, California, offer Sunday evening services, which in many cases are the most heavily attended services of the week. Other churches have had success offering services on Friday and Saturday nights. As the demand for more time with family increases for boomers in the '90s, the 10:00 A.M. Sunday service will have a harder time attracting new people.

Single-parent families face the same difficulties as split-parent families and continue to be a growing segment of our population. The 1990 census showed that the number of single parents had increased 2.8 million since 1980 to a total of 9.7 million. While the growth was at a slower rate than in the '70s, this was an almost 30 percent increase. Other census results showed that women with no husband present maintained 44 percent of African-American households, compared to 13 percent for Euro-American households, and 23 percent for Hispanic-American households.[14]

The significance of these findings is that single-parent families are making up a larger share of those who take care of children. Other reports show that the poorest people of our nation are found among mother-only families who make up half of the nation's poor. Sixty percent of those under the poverty line are women, and the majority of them are Euro-American.[15] Of the 33 million poor Americans, 13 million are children, and 500,000 of those children are homeless.[16]

As boomers rediscover the family, the issues of how to take care of poor children, of providing adequate daycare for all families, of providing quality education for rich and poor alike, of teaching children values that last, of providing resources to help the most vulnerable in our society—all will be at the top of the nation's agenda. The results from a 1989 poll conducted by *Time/CNN*, drives home the point. When asked what was the most important issue for women, number one was helping women balance work and family. Number two was getting government funding for programs such as childcare and maternity leave.

Multiculturalism

The watchword for the '90s will be multiculturalism—the concept of looking at the world through the eyes of more than one culture. As the percentage of ethnic minorities grows, the challenge to boomers will be maintaining their cultural identity while at the same time affirming the identity of others. The first to embrace this idea are educators who have been forced by sheer numbers to reevaluate educational curriculum in light of the growth of ethnic minorities in their schools. In large states such as California, New York, Florida, and Texas, educators have been challenged to develop understanding among diverse ethnic groups. In Los Angeles more than ninety different languages are spoken by school children. The University of California at Irvine reported that over 50 percent of its 1991 freshman class was Asian. For the first time in its history, an ethnic "minority" became a majority.

Whereas in 1916 the term *melting pot* was coined to describe the assimilation of newcomers into North American society, multiculturalism best describes what's happening to the American population now. The year 2056 will find the average U.S. resident tracing his/her roots to Africa, Asia, Hispanic countries, the Pacific Islands, Arabia—everywhere except Europe.[17]

Not just education will be affected by these changes. In the workplace an equally profound adjustment will have to be made for companies that wish to compete in the global marketplace. In 1988 the labor force was divided as follows: 41 percent native Euro-American males, 33 percent native Euro-American females, 10 percent native minority males, 9 percent native minority females, 4 percent immigrant males, and 3 percent immigrant females. But the makeup of those entering the workforce from 1988 to 2000 will be quite different. Only 9 percent of new workers will be native Euro-American males. The rest will be 28 percent native Euro-American females, 21 percent native minority males, 21 percent native minority males, 21 percent native minority females, 12 percent immigrant males, and 9 percent immigrant females.[18]

While today the United States corporate world is dominated by Euro-American males, by 2000 a huge shift in demographics will have taken place. Women and minorities will have moved into position to share in the decision-making power of the American business world. Colgate-Palmolive's chairperson, Reuben Mark, has embraced cultural diversity as a company goal. Since 1986 women have gone from comprising 9 percent to comprising 25 percent of its managers. Rather than seeing women and minorities as a hindrance, Mark sees them as a new and flexible resource. Because the company does business in sixty countries, the concept of multiculturalism is seen as a way to boost sales and to motivate new managers.[19]

Churches in the San Gabriel Valley, just outside of Los Angeles, have seen the immigrant population rise dramatically in the last ten years. While some churches have closed their doors, others have opened their doors to new ethnic ministries, which have given their churches new life. Alhambra First United Methodist Church has three language congregations—Chinese, Korean, and English—as well as Asbury United Methodist Church, a Filipino church, sharing the same facility. By incorporating these groups into one facility, the church has a new focus in ministry and hope for the future.

The most delicate question relating to multiculturalism has to do with the present ethnic majority's willingness to share power and to pave the way for a positive future. Euro-Americans, as a whole, do not have the same cultural identity as other ethnic groups, because as members of the majority they have seen themselves as being "the Americans." But in a culturally and ethnically diverse population, the Euro-American will have to redefine his or her cultural identity. It never ceases to amaze me that when I ask Euro-American boomers or their children what their ethnic heritage is, I commonly receive a blank stare for an answer. Although their roots are found in the rich and diverse culture of the European continent, they have little realization of the important heritage they bring to the North American scene.

Multiculturalism will benefit not only the U.S. citizen with African, Asian, Arabian, or Hispanic roots; it also will allow Euro-Americans to find a place in the new, multicultured North American tapestry. Boomers of all ethnic groups will preside over these changes as they move into places of leadership. Their choices will shape the ability of the United States to compete in the global marketplace and will either encourage or hinder the development of a new North American society in the next country.

Supernatural Spirituality

The movie *Ghost* surprised Hollywood when it became the number one movie of the 1990 summer season. Big budget movies such as *Robocop II* and sequels such as *Three Men and a Little Lady* were expected to rake in the dough. But *Ghost*, the story of two lovers separated by murder and reunited through a channeler, hit the top. Later in 1991 when it was released on video, it went to number one again. Even more surprising, Whoopi Goldberg, who played the channeler, won the Oscar for best supporting actress. That the role of a medium who was able to communicate with the dead at seances was believable enough to win an award for a dramatic role says a lot about our religious beliefs.

In April 1991, *American Demographics* reported the results of a Gallup Poll that showed that people between the ages of thirty and forty-nine are the most likely to believe in paranormal phenomena. Of all U.S. adults 55 percent believe in devils, a 39 percent increase since 1978, while at the same time belief in ghosts increased from 11 percent to 25 percent of all adults. Furthermore, 71 percent said they believe in life after death. These beliefs were equally high in the religious and nonreligious populations.[20]

The Day America Told the Truth, the poll based on an extensive survey of U.S. citizens taken in October 1990, reported even higher numbers of belief in the paranormal: 45 percent believe in ghosts; 31 percent believe that some people have magical powers; 28 percent believe in witchcraft; and as many as one in twenty have actually participated in some ritual of Satanism or witchcraft.[21]

These findings are borne out by the fastest-selling book in the Christian market, *This Present Darkness.* This novel by Frank E. Peretti had sold over 1.5 million copies and over 43,000 audiotape versions by March 1991. Scott Young of Crossway Books, the publisher of this bestseller, says the audiotape is being syndicated in half-hour slots to 165 radio stations across the country and plans are to release it as a major motion picture in 1993.

The book recounts the lives of the people of Ashton, who find themselves in the midst of a spiritual battle between angels and demons when a New Age plot to subjugate the entire human race is hatched in their town. One scene describes the arrival of Tal, the angel who is the Captain of the Host, who has come to do battle with Rafar, the Prince of Babylon.

> Yes, it was indeed Tal, the Captain of the Host. It was so strange to see this mighty warrior standing in this humble little place. Guilo had seen him near the throne room of Heaven itself, in conference with none other than Michael. But here he stood the same impressive figure with golden hair and ruddy complexion, intense golden eyes like fire and an unchallengeable air of authority. . . .
>
> No warrior Guilo had ever seen could fight as Tal could; no demon could outmaneuver or outspeed him, no sword could parry a blow from the sword of Tal. Side by side, Guilo and his captain had vanquished demonic powers for as long as those rebels existed and had been companions in the Lord's service before there had been any rebellion at all.[22]

This story of angelic warriors doing battle against the demonic forces of evil is a motif that has captured the imagination of baby boomer Christians. When asked why he thought the book was recording such phenomenal sales, Young replied that "in the last few years Christians have come to an increased awareness of the spiritual side of their lives, that their actions, beliefs, and thoughts have an impact in the supernatural world. This is especially seen in a person's prayer life."[23]

This Present Darkness and *Ghost* serve as two examples of the supernatural spirituality that will remain popular throughout the '90s. Although many have said that the New Age is passé, its theology remains an influence in the media, the workplace, and the schools. While *This Present Darkness* is a refutation of the New Age from one Christian perspective, the continuing desire of boomers to explore new vistas of spirituality will continue.

Churches that take these beliefs and concerns seriously will have the best chance to speak to this generation. To ignore them is to put oneself out of the religious debate that is raging in the American religious subculture. The mix of millennialism and supernaturalism will become a heady brew by 2000, and churches will become a place to calm people's fears and to help them put their beliefs in perspective. Even more critical will be the need to offer a spirituality that includes discipleship and growth to enable people to mature in their faith.

The Age Wave

One baby boomer in her late twenties told me, "My friends and I are now getting older and we are beginning to think about other things, like God, and taking care of our children, and being responsible adults."

This realization of growing older brings with it a need for security, for beyond the threats of the nuclear age comes a new fear: facing one's own mortality. It is ironic that the "Don't trust anyone over thirty" generation will have the most impact on U.S. culture and society as it comes of age in the '90s. In *Age Wave*, Ken Dychtwald and Joe Flower write:

> The senior boom, the birth dearth, and the aging of the baby boom are coming together to create a massive demographic shift, one which we refer to as the Age Wave. The numbers themselves will peak in the early decades of the new century as the baby boomers reach their fifties, sixties, and seventies. But the shift in attitudes, style, and meaning—"the social revolution" that the Age Wave brings—will begin to rumble and quake long before the first boomer turns 65.[24]

This age wave has great implications for the baby boom generation. Already there are more people over sixty-five years of age than ever before, but today's numbers will pale in comparison to those of the future. When this huge demographic bulge hits retirement, government services will be stretched to the limit, medical costs will soar, and housing to meet the needs of infirm seniors will be at a premium. Cheryl Russell in *100 Predications for the Baby Boom* says:

> In middle age, the huge size of the baby-boom generation will work in its favor. In old age, its huge size could crush it. The well-being of baby boomers in old age depends on their breaking away from the crowd and provisioning themselves for survival as their health fails. Those who stock up well with money and family will enjoy their leisure years. Those who don't will have to depend on the good will of a society that finds the baby boom a burden, and on the compassion of younger people who live in the baby boom's shadow. Most baby boomers are not used to being poor, but many may be poor in old age.[25]

The main problem facing boomers in the next century is numbers. Immediately following the boomers is a group of demographers call the "baby bust." Between 1965 and 1976, there was an 18 percent drop in births in comparison to the previous twelve years. Since 1946 the highest number of births recorded in a year was 4,332,000 in 1957, during the height of the baby boom, but the lowest number of births was in 1973 when 3,168,000 babies were born. That's a staggering difference of 1,164,000 babies.[26] No wonder fast-food restaurants and employers in general are worried because of the drop in available workers in that age group.

Even though boomers are rediscovering the family, they are still not replacing themselves. It is expected that as many as one-third of boomers will remain childless or have only one child. A long-term implication of this is that when baby boomers begin to face debilitating diseases that come with old age, a large portion of them will not have children to take care of them.

Another result of the lower birthrate will be a smaller work force, which will not have the resources to fund Social Security as we know it. When Social Security was formed in 1935, life expectancy was age sixty-three. Now more than 30 million people are over sixty-five and this group is increasing by 6 million every decade.[27]

In 1935 there were more than forty workers contributing to Social Security for each retired person; by 1950 the number of contributors had shrunk to seventeen. In the 1990s it will go down to 3.4, and by 2020 the support ratio will be 1.78 to 1.[28] In an article entitled "Bad News for Baby Boomers," Matthew Greenwald warns boomers to act now so they can stay away from the poorhouse in the next century.[29]

One of the chief difficulties will be the cutback in Social Security for baby boomers. A typical worker earning $40,000 a year in 2010 would have to pay $8,000 in Social Security taxes, while a typical business grossing $1 million would have to pay $200,000 in Social Security taxes to fund the Social Security system as it now stands.

According to the board of trustees of the Medicare Hospital Insurance Trust Fund, this trust fund is projected to be insolvent before 2011. Others estimate that the Social Security fund will go broke in 2025. Another troublesome trend is the use of Social Security surplus to offset the federal deficit.[30] The writing on the wall is clear: Boomers should not expect to receive much, if any, help from Medicare or Social Security when they reach retirement.

If the federal government and the family are not able to take care of baby boomers when they hit their senior years, community services will have to fill in the gap. Churches, synagogues, hospitals, and organizations such as the Red Cross and the Salvation Army will be on the front line in the battle to provide the necessary assistance boomers are going to need. Local city and county governments will have to form a partnership with these volunteer organizations to help fund senior nutrition programs, emergency medical care, housing projects, and senior daycare. These are the minimal services that will be needed to take care of the more than 67 million seniors who will make up over 21 percent of the population by the year 2050.[31] These organizations should be putting such programs in action now to prepare for the rising tide of seniors who will be in need in the next century.

The flip side of the age wave is a boom in health and fitness. Whether it is diet plans, fitness clubs and exercise gyms, or skin-care products and bifocal glasses, the aging of the baby boom will bring with it goods and services that will cater to the boomers' desire to stay young. An example of this is seen in the exploding sales of home exercise equipment, which sold $2 billion in 1990, three times the sales of 1980. One of the hottest items is the Stairclimber, a low-impact exercise machine that conditions the whole body.

Entrepreneur reports that the home fitness market has seen rapid growth in three areas: personal training, equipment, and exercise videocassettes. Thomas Doyle of the National Sporting Goods Association cites the baby boomers who are moving into middle age as the cause for the tremendous growth in this market. Because they are more fitness-oriented and have higher expectations for their physical well-being than their parents' generation, continued growth can be counted on in the coming years.

As boomers move into their senior years in the next century, they will be sure to leave their mark. The wise boomer should be planning now for the future, and those who desire to reach this generation should be making plans as to how to stay in touch with this generation as it moves into its next phase of life.

The Experience Quest

The information age brings with it a set of needs and concerns that are different from those of the past. Whereas the industrial revolution has satisfied most people's requirements for tangible goods such as cars, housing, and clothing, the challenge of the information age is to meet baby boomers' desire for richer experiences. In an article titled "Experience Industry" James Ogilvy explains that this industry includes such things as exercise videotapes, big salaries for those who entertain us, drug money, our electronic entertainment, and the money we pay for "quasi-spiritual" experiences.[32]

This experience quest will be amplified as new information-based products hit the market. For example, products based on virtual reality, the interaction of a person in a computer-based environment, will make today's generation of television and video games look like antiques. By putting on goggles hooked to a computer, a person can walk and move in a simulated environment created by a computer. In this environment people can open doors, go up stairs, and throw balls to a computer-generated character. While the outside observer sees a lone individual making strange moves in an empty room, the participant finds him or herself immersed in a sensual and active world projected through the headgear.

Whether someone is tying a bungee cord around the waist and jumping out of a balloon, is engrossed in the next best-seller, or is flipping through 100 channels on the television, the experience quest will typify information age living in the '90s. This trend seeks to satisfy the needs and desires of the individual. It is focused on developing skills, on escaping the rigors of everyday living, and on creating a whole new you.

In the business world some are calling the 1990s the "decade of the customer." In a *Business Week* cover story on "King Customer" it was reported that customer service is considered very important by managers because they know good service will attract many customers and much money. Managers from a wide range of businesses are considering reworking entire organizations around giving customers what they want.[33]

The reason for this focus on the customer is that customers have become choosier about what they want. Instead of remaining loyal to a brand name, they are continually seeking products that best meet their standards and needs. If a Ford does not offer them the experience they want when they drive a car, they have no compunctions about switching to a Toyota, which gives them all the luxury and performance they expect in a car. This choosiness is especially true of the baby boom generation, which has high expectations for the service they receive and for the quality of the products they buy. Anna Quindlen, a thirty-five-year-old baby boomer, wife, and mother of two, explains that her mother's generation wanted convenience, but baby boomers want things that last. This generation also prefers high-tech products, which perform better.[34]

Another need that comes from the experience quest is the desire to "do it yourself." Boomers want to participate in life and actively look for programs and methods to help develop themselves. Colleges are finding a huge market in continuing education courses for boomers who have already received a degree but desire to continue their education. To stay abreast of the rapid changes of the information age, most professionals—from doctors to lawyers, from teachers to pastors—require continuing education.

When we translate these needs to the church, we can see why a lot of churches are having problems attracting the baby boom generation. Although there are 77 million baby boomers, 50 million of them do not go to church. This is based on Gallup's findings that 34 percent of boomers attend church. Although 65 percent say they are church members, a more solid percentage of boomers who take the church seriously is based on worship attendance.[35] *The Day America Told the Truth* paints an even bleaker picture:

What is going on in congregations, parishes, and synagogues across America? The news is good—and bad. God is alive and very well. But right now in America, fewer people are listening to what God has to say than ever before. Ninety percent of the people we questioned said that they truly believe in God.

It would be the logical conclusion then to think that God is a meaningful factor in today's America. But we reached a different conclusion when we dug deeper with our questions. . . . When we asked how people make up their minds on issues of right and wrong, we found that they simply do not turn to God or religion to help them decide about the seminal or moral issues of the day. . . .

As we enter the 1990s, only one American in five ever consults a minister, a priest, or a rabbi on everyday issues. Half of us haven't been to a religious service for a minimum of three months. One in three haven't been to a religious service for more than a year. More than half of us (58 percent) went to services regularly while growing up, but less than half of those (27 percent) do so today.[36]

For churches to attract and keep baby boomers they have to offer four things that relate to the experience quest. First, they must offer a rich experience of worship. Boomers do not want to be observers of worship; they want to be active participants. Many nondenominational churches find it far easier to recognize changing needs and demands than do monolithic denominations whose changes must go through the hierarchy of bureaucracy. These new-style churches have done the unthinkable to the older generation: They have scrapped the choir and replaced it with lively, upbeat congregational singing led by a music group using guitars, synthesizers, and drums. Some even go so far as to write their own songs, which enhance their brand of theology. The result is that worshipers have the experience of singing in full voice, over an extended time, and do not feel constrained by pews. Standing, clapping, and raising hands is an accepted practice in these churches.

Second, boomers expect customer service, especially in regard to their children. A clean, well-kept, organized Sunday school is imperative in order to keep baby boomers. As many have said, the most important room in the church is the nursery. If it is dingy, with cribs falling apart and two giggling youth in charge, boomer parents will not leave their precious children in such an undesirable environment.

Customer relations has to do with such things as the way people are greeted at the door and the quality of the bulletins and the church newsletter, and the follow-up of visitors. Boomers respond only to things that are done first-class. They receive it everywhere else, so why shouldn't they receive it at church?

Third, boomers want to be informed. When they come to worship they do not want to hear a lecture on theology. They want practical, down-to-earth advice about how to make it through the next week. Many churches meet this need by providing sermon notes on which worshipers write down insights and thoughts as the pastor gives the message. Also, churches that retain boomers offer a wide variety of classes and seminars, which help them develop and identify their own ministry. Chief among the teachings in these churches is a strong emphasis on spiritual gifts, which help each discover the spiritual gift or gifts that God has given to that person.

Fourth, boomers do not respond well to the pastor who thinks he or she has to do it all alone. Pastors who are able to delegate, train, and build up believers are the ones who succeed in the information age.

C. Peter Wagner, professor of church growth at Fuller Theological Seminary, gives us an indication of what churches that retain baby boomers offer. He says that "boomer churches are retaining their members because they have multiple ways of making the baby boomers perceive that their needs are being met—more participatory worship, contemporary musicology, a power dimension, systems of networking, opening doors to ministry where people feel like they are making a difference, large churches with more options—those kinds of things are providing more than what the traditional county-seat, mainline local church has offered in the past."[37]

The experience quest will test the limits of morality, individuality, and practicality as more products roll off the information age assembly line. Boomers and their children will be faced with many choices that will eat at their time together and challenge the strength of their relationships. But with a vision of wholeness, these products and choices can enhance, build, and create experiences of wonder and joy unimaginable to any previous generation. The ability to communicate, to share, and to learn has never been at a higher level in human society. Boomers will have the opportunity to use these resources to build a better and more equitable society. Their choices will shape the world for generations to come.

Networking

The biggest dream of the typical baby boomer is not to be the company president; it is to be his/her own boss. Bill Bray, a forty-two-year-old boomer, has come to the conclusion that economic security lies in going into business for himself. But how can he do this without putting his family at risk? Recently he happened onto one of the growing trends of the '90s, networking. He discovered that by tapping into his network of friends, relatives, and neighbors, the possibility of developing his own business was in reach. So he became a distributor for Amway, the largest multilevel marketing company in this country, whose $2.2 billion in sales in 1990 more than doubled the 1980 figure and is expected to jump to higher levels into the '90s.

Why did he go in this direction? Bray says, "The primary reason is financial. It's hard to depend on the construction industry, which has been so undependable. If this works out, I won't be working for the other guy—I will be able to schedule my own hours and have more time for my family."[38]

An Amway distributor not only has 400 Amway products plus a personal shoppers' catalog containing over 5,000 brand-name products to offer to customers; he/she also can take advantage of distributor incentives—by signing up new distributors and sharing in their profits as they expand their business.

Amway's method has proven so successful in Japan that by 1989, Japan had over 500,000 Amway distributors. Amway's $500 million in sales made it the ninth-most-profitable foreign-owned company in Japan. One of the secrets of that success is that the direct selling approach has proven to be a great way to circumvent Japan's restrictive and costly distribution system.[39]

This one-to-one approach is what makes networking a trend for the '90s. Boomers, always an independent lot, are looking for freedom and economic security. They do not want to trust their future to anyone but themselves.

Jason Chaffetz, spokesperson for Nu Skin, another multilevel company whose number of distributors has grown from 50,000 to 100,000 in the last two years, says,

> Our primary market is Baby Boomers. We sell superior skin and hair care products that attract equal numbers of men and women who want to stay young and healthy. Boomers are also attracted to our marketing strategy which allows them to make an extra $100 to $200 or more a month, which can make a big difference for the family income. Since our company opened in 1984 we have sold hundreds of millions of dollars worth of products.

Businesses are not the only ones who are catching on to this trend. In fact, the fastest-growing churches in the '90s will be those that network through the development of small groups. Carl F. George, director of the Charles E. Fuller Institute, has developed a new model for the church based on networking, which he calls the "meta-church." With information-based technology and the desire of Christians to develop their own ministry, the meta-church model lays the groundwork for developing leaders to head small groups in the church.

The pastor-in-charge is seen as the trainer whose main goal is to develop leaders for small groups. They in turn discover and train new leaders for new small groups. Rather than ministry taking place on Sunday mornings, the real ministry takes place as members of small groups care, encourage, and pray for one another. The small group becomes the place where faith is developed as members discover and use their spiritual gifts.[40]

Networking in the church has unlimited potential because the focus is on developing small groups of eight to twelve people who can meet anywhere. Churches that are more concerned about the unchurched harvest than they are with simply filling their buildings will be the ones that will grow the Body of Christ and disciple the new Christians of the future.

Serendipity House, which publishes a wide range of small group studies for the Christian community, has seen requests for its seminars "go through the roof," according to Mickey Elliot, a staff person at the company. Over thirty years' time Lyman Coleman, Serendipity's founder, has trained more than 200,000 pastors in his small group techniques. Elliot says the goal of these studies is "to help people turn felt needs into shared values so the walking wounded can become wounded healers." Like George, Elliot sees a tremendous growth in small group ministries designed to equip people to grow and share their faith in meaningful ways.[41]

Networking taps into the baby boomer generation's desire for personal contact, sharing, companionship, and—paradoxically—independence. Whether in business or in faith, small groups will have the power to expand and grow in a society that is hungry for relationships. Churches that provide resources and tools for developing these relationships are the ones that will reach those who are tired of the nagging loneliness that plagues much of their lives.

The Simple Life

Rather than focus on individual segments of life, boomers want a life that takes in all its parts. The superwoman who wants it all plays many roles: the adoring wife, the loving mother, the tough boss, the smart businesswoman, the caring child, the adept housekeeper, and the ardent lover. But jumping from role to role and from place to place brings with it a feeling of constantly being in chaos. Where does one put down one's feet? Where does one find rest and peace? Where is the meaning in all that one does?

This questioning of one's role in life, looking for the meaning behind the rush and bustle of modern life, is leading boomers to the simple life. Tired of the results of the trendy materialistic '80s and unable to keep up financially with the Joneses of past fame, they are looking for basic values that last.

A *Times/CNN* poll taken early in 1991 showed a nationwide shift in the need of personal agendas. Sixty-nine percent said they would like to slow down to live a more relaxed life versus 19 percent who wanted a faster-paced, exciting life. Eighty-nine percent said it was more important to spend time with their families than to do anything else. For many this desire is seen in having time to be with family and friends, to rest and enjoy recreation, to do good deeds, to help save the environment, and to develop one's own spirituality.[42]

Most commentators on the scene say that as boomers age in the 1990s, they will return to religion as a way to sort through their spiritual values as they pursue the simple life. The question for the Christian church is whether or not boomers will stay. Most boomers will give the church only one more try.

Churches that do not address the felt needs of boomers will lose out. Those who come across as anti-everything will be hard-pressed to minister to a group that has tried it all and is looking for some way to make sense of what they have been through. When boomers come through the doors of a church, they already know their "sins." They know how they have fallen short. What they need is a loving place where they can begin to put their lives back together.

The presuppositions of baby boomers about life are much different from those of their parents' generation. They are not concerned about dress, etiquette, or even being "moral" in the traditional sense of the word. Most couples have lived together before being married or are living together now. The sins they are dealing with are the sins of broken relationships between lovers, between parent and child, between themselves and God, between humanity and the created world. What they are looking for is wholeness.

Wholeness means that a person is part of a community, a community of people who care for one another, a community that offers freedom of development, the discipline of being accountable to others, and the balance of mind, body, head, and heart. Wholeness is also found as a person lives out faith in relationship to God. For the church to offer wholeness it must be a community, not an institution.

This community is firmly based in an authentic Christian spirituality that not only talks about faith but also puts it into action. The touchstone of the community is the belief that the God who brings salvation through Jesus Christ also calls believers to share this salvation with the world. Instead of focusing on divisive labels, such as *liberal, evangelical, fundamentalist,* and *charismatic,* the spirituality of wholeness calls believers to a new Christian worldview that focuses on two things: personal faith and justice.

Personal faith is lived out in relationship to God and in relationship to the community of believers. This faith is nourished and developed through the Holy Spirit, which enables the believer to use his or her gifts for the whole Body of Christ.

Justice calls the community to be accountable for its actions, to be witnesses to the world for peace and love, to bring the liberating news of Jesus to the world, to be an ethical community from which and in which right and wrong can be judged through the wisdom of God.

Rather than a mechanistic view of spirituality based on moralisms—do not drink, do not smoke, do not dance, do not pollute—wholeness is based on the biological view that life is imbued with the Spirit of God which causes believers to be moral as a result of God's working in their lives.

True spirituality is that which is in connection with God, with the creation, and with people, as believers seek to live out their lives. A complete awareness of God's presence—as seen in the created world from the flowers to the trees, from the fish to the birds of the air, from the child at play to the senior near death—brings to one a sense of the wholeness of life, an understanding that through God all things are formed and because of God all things have life.

This desire for wholeness has boomers searching in some surprising places. Peter Drucker says that the largest employer in the country is the third sector of the economy. What exactly is the third sector? It is the sector of our society that puts to work the large populace of volunteers who are found in its churches, hospitals, support groups, museums, symphony orchestras, Scouts, and organizations such as the Red Cross. One out of every two adult Americans, a total of 90 million people, are estimated to work as volunteers in the third sector in addition to holding down a paid job.[43] An additional 100 million say they are ready to volunteer, especially to help prevent child abuse (50 percent), to rebuild the American education system (41 percent), and to help save the environment (29 percent).[44]

These volunteers put in the equivalent of 7.5 million full-time work years. If they were paid, their wages would amount to $150 billion a year. Drucker says that the one thing they have in common is "that their purpose is to change human beings. The product of the hospital is a cured patient, the product of a church is a changed life."[45]

The importance of the third sector in American life is that it brings its citizens together. The laborer and the knowledge worker, the house-wife/husband and the businessperson, the student and the teacher, the African-American and Euro-American, the rich and the poor—all find common cause in volunteering to be change agents. The third sector provides the new bonds of community and a sphere of meaningful citizenship that is characterized by the simple life virtue of giving to others.

Now that the size and complexity of government make direct participation all but impossible, it is the human-change institution of the third sector that is offering its volunteers a sphere of personal achievement in which the individual exercises influence, discharges responsibility, and makes decisions. . . . In the political culture of mainstream society, individuals, no matter how well educated, how successful, how achieving, or how wealthy, can only vote and pay taxes. They can only react, can only be passive. In the counterculture of the third sector, they are active citizens. This may be the most important contribution of the third sector. So far it is a purely American achievement.[46]

The trends and movements of the American culture that have shaped and moved the baby boom generation are now asking this generation to be its leaders. The boomer legacy will depend on a willingness to join together to be in community, to make commitments to relationships, to work toward justice and freedom, to be willing to sacrifice in order to save the environment and protect America's future, and to respect the beliefs and perspectives of other people and their cultures.

In this regard, *Baby Boomer Spirituality* gives us a starting place, and something of a roadmap, for walking into the future. We have been reminded that the values and beliefs we hold affect the whole of our lives—relationships, work, goals, faith, and most fundamentally, our self-understanding. It is not enough just to wander through life on a yellow brick road that leads to nowhere. Instead, each of us must be challenged to look anew at life and to ask, "What difference for good can I make in the world?" Each of us must be challenged to willingly inquire, "God, what are you calling me to do?"

The other day I walked into the nursery to see what was, for me, a scene of beauty. My mom and wife were huddled over my five-week-old daughter as they finished her bath. As I looked at them I saw the seasons of change spread over the years; from the earliest memories of my mother who can remember life before television, microwave dinners, and VCRs, who carries with her the simple virtues of her Scandinavian parents who came to the United States in the early 1900s, survived a San Francisco earthquake, and raised their children during the Depression; to the strength, care, and compassion of my wife who carries with her the memories of a global child, born in Canton China and raised in Hong Kong; to my daughter, whose dreams will be realized in a future full of peril and promise.

As I thought of my place in their world, I wondered what it was that bound us together so tightly. Was it happenstance, an instant in time, a fluke of nature? Or was it more than that? What dawned on me at that moment was that it was love that held us together, a love deeply rooted in God. Perhaps that is the best place to end and to start, with the simple basic truth that is at the heart of the best spritualty: God loves us all.

RECOMMENDED READING

Campbell, Joseph and Bill Moyers. *The Power of Myth.* New York: Doubleday, 1988.

Chandler, Russell. *Understanding the New Age.* Dallas: Word Publishing, 1988.

Drucker, Peter F. *The New Realities.* New York: Harper & Row, Publishers, 1989.

Dychtwald, Ken and James Flower. *Age Wave.* Los Angeles: Jeremy P. Tarcher, Inc., 1989.

Fallow, James. *More Like Us, Making America Great Again.* Boston: Houghton Mifflin Company, 1989.

Ferguson, Marilyn. *The Aquarian Conspiracy.* Los Angeles: J. P. Tarcher, Inc., 1980.

Gallup, Jr. George and Jim Castelli. *The People's Religion.* New York: Macmillan Publishing Company, 1990.

Gitlin, Todd. *The Sixties: Years of Hope, Days of Rage.* New York: Bantam Books, 1987.

Gottlieb, Annie. *Do You Believe In Magic? The Second Coming of the Sixties Generation.* New York: Times Books, 1987.

Kaiser, Charles. *1968 in America.* New York: Weidenfeld & Nicolson, 1988.

Littwin, Susan. *The Postponed Generation: Why American Youth Are Growing Up Later.* New York: William Morrow and Company, Inc., 1986.

Palmer, Laura. *Shrapnel in the Heart.* New York: Vintage Books, 1988.

Patterson, James and Peter Kim. *The Day America Told the Truth.* New York: Prentice-Hall Press, 1991.

Troeger, Thomas H. *Imagining a Sermon.* Nashville: Abingdon Press, 1990.

Weiss, Michael J. *The Clustering of America.* New York: Harper & Row, Publishers, 1988.

ENDNOTES

Chapter 1

1. Aimee I. Stern, "The Baby Boomers Are Richer and Older," *Business Month*, October 1987, p. 24. Reprinted with permission, *Business Month* Magazine (Oct. 1987) Copyright © 1987, by Goldhirsh Group, Inc., 38 Commercial Wharf, Boston, MA 02110.

2. Peter H. Brown and Steven Gaines, *The Love You Make, An Insider's Story of the Beatles* (New York: Signet Books, 1984), pp. 97 and 104.

3. Henry Hurt, *Reasonable Doubt* (New York: Holt, Rinehart and Winston, 1985), pp. 21-22.

4. Harris Survey, April 2, 1985; *Washington Post*, November 20, 1983.

5. Kurt Anderson, "Hot Mood," *Rolling Stone*, May 18, 1989, p. 58. By Straight Arrow Publishers, Inc. © 1988. All rights reserved. Reprinted by permission.

6. Tom Shachtman, *Decade of Shocks* (New York: Poseidon Press, 1983), pp. 22-30.

7. Theodore H. White, *America in Search of Itself* (New York: Harper & Row, Publishers, 1982), p. 7.

8. Shachtman, pp. 49-50.

9. Annie Gottlieb, *"Do You Believe in Magic? The Second Coming of the Sixties Generation"* (New York: Times Books, 1987), p. 10.

10. Ibid., p. 11.

11. Stern, p. 24.

12. Sandra Tsing Loh, "Homefront," *Los Angeles Times Magazine*, April 14, 1991, p. 7.

13. Katy Butler, "The Great Boomer Depression," *Mother Jones*, June 1989, p. 34. © 1989 by Katy Butler. Reprinted by permission.

14. Kirk McNeill and Robert Paul, *Reaching for the Baby Boomers Workbook* (Nashville, Tennessee: The General Board of Discipleship of The United Methodist Church, 1989), p. 24.

15. Susan Chace, "My Generation," *Seventeen*, October 1989, p. 100.

16. Stanley Karnow, *Vietnam, A History* (New York: Penguin Books, 1983), p. 46.

17. Laura Palmer, *Shrapnel in the Heart* (New York: Vintage Books, 1988), p. xiv.

18. Martin Anderson, "America Can Now Claim a Warrior Class," *Los Angeles Times*, April 7, 1991, p. M5.

19. Palmer, pp. 12-13.

20. Ibid., p. 17.

21. Ibid., p. 15.

22. William Greider, "Rolling Stone Survey," *Rolling Stone*, April 7, 1988, p. 36. By Straight Arrow Publishers, Inc. © 1989. All rights reserved. Reprinted by permission.

23. Palmer, p. xii.

Chapter 2

1. Kathryn A. London and Barbara Foley Wilson, "Divorce," *American Demographics*, October 1988, p. 23.

2. Ibid., p. 57.

3. Ibid.

4. David Bloom, "Childless Couples," *American Demographics*, August 1986, p. 23.

5. Ken Dychtwald and Joe Flower, *Age Wave* (Los Angeles: Jeremy P. Tarcher, Inc., 1989), p. 11.

6. David Sheff, "Portrait of a Generation," *Rolling Stone*, May 5, 1988, pp. 49-50.

7. Susan Littwin, *The Postponed Generation: Why American Youth Are Growing Up Later* (New York: William Morrow and Company, Inc., 1986), p. 215.

8. *Book of Worship* (Nashville, Tennessee: The Methodist Publishing House, 1964), p. 29.

9. Sheff, p. 49.

10. Robert S. Weiss, *Loneliness: The Experience of Emotional and Social Isolation* (Cambridge, Massachusetts: MIT Press, 1973), p. 1.

11. Ibid., p. 1.

12. Ibid., p. 10.

13. Ibid., p. 14.

14. Letitia Anne Peplau and Daniel Perlman, *Loneliness: A Sourcebook of Current Theory, Research and Therapy* (New York: John Wiley & Sons, 1982), pp. 172-74.

15. Ibid., p. 172.

16. Claudia Wallis, "Onward, Women!," *Time*, December 4, 1989, p. 89.

17. "Time and Togetherness," *Psychology Today*, January 1988, p. 10.

18. Wallis, p. 86.

19. "The Housework Gap," *Psychology Today*, January 10, 1988, p. 10.

20. Wallis, p. 89.

21. Ibid., p. 86.

22. Judith Waldrop, "Who Are the Caregivers?," *American Demographics*, September 1989, p. 39.

23. David Sheff, "What Really Matters," *Rolling Stone*, May 5, 1988, p. 53.

24. Peplau and Perlman, p. 172.

25. Sheff, "What Really Matters," *Rolling Stone*, May 5, 1988, p. 54.

26. Peplau and Perlman, p. 172.

27. "Loneliness as an American Epidemic," *U.S. News & World Report*, July 21, 1986. Used by permission.

28. Peplau and Perlman, p. 172.

29. David Sheff, "Sex, Drugs, and Rock 'n' Roll," *Rolling Stone*, May 5, 1988, p. 58.

30. Suzanne M. Bianchi and Judith A. Seltzer, "Life Without Father," *American Demographics*, December 1986, p. 43. Reprinted with permission. © American Demographics (Dec. 1986).

31. Cheryl Russell, *100 Predictions for the Baby Boom* (New York: Penum Press, 1987), p. 206.

32. Peplau and Perlman, p. 174.

33. Littwin, pp. 15-16.

34. *American Demographics*, May 1987, p. 14.

35. Katy Butler, "The Great Boomer Depression," *Mother Jones*, June 1989, p. 34.

36. Littwin, p. 16.

37. Ibid., p. 52.

38. Dan Kiley, *Living Together, Feeling Alone* (New York: Prentice Hall Press, 1989), p. 3.

39. Ibid., pp. 4-5.

40. Ibid., p. 23.

41. Ibid., pp. 4-5.

42. Wallis, p. 82.

43. Kiley, p. 13.

44. Weiss, p. 19.

Chapter 3

1. Annie Gottlieb, *Do You Believe in Magic?* (New York: Time Books, 1987), p. 84.

2. Midge Decter, *Liberal Parents, Radical Children* (New York: Coward, McCann & Geoghegan, Inc., 1975), p. 27.

3. Peter F. Drucker, *The New Realities* (New York: Harper & Row, Publishers, 1989), pp. 188-90.

4. Michael J. Weiss, *The Clustering of America* (New York: Harper & Row, Publishers, 1988), p. 170.

5. Barbara Ehrenreich, *Fear of Falling: The Inner Life of the Middle Class* (New York: Pantheon Books, 1989), pp. 227-28.

6. Ibid., p. 37.

7. Ibid.

8. Ken Dychtwald and Joe Flower, *Age Wave* (Los Angeles: Jeremy P. Tarcher, Inc., 1989), p. 15.

9. Ehrenreich, p. 92.

10. Charles Kaiser, *1968 in America* (New York: Weidenfeld & Nicolson, 1988), p. 191.

11. Todd Gitlin, *The Sixties: Years of Hope, Days of Rage* (New York: Bantam Books, 1987), p. 199.

12. Ibid., pp. 196-201.

13. Ibid., p. 201.

14. Gottlieb, p. 169.

15. Peter Brown and Steven Gaines, *The Love You Make: An Insider's Story of the Beatles* (New York: Signet Books, 1983), pp. 143-44.

16. Gottlieb, p. 175.

17. Charles Perry, *The Haight-Ashbury* (New York: Vintage Books, 1985), p. 122.

18. Ibid., p. 95.

19. Ibid., p. 130.

20. Gitlin, p. 206.

21. Ibid., pp. 205-06.

22. Brown and Gaines, p. 181.

23. Ibid., p. 222.

24. Ibid., p. 221.

25. "Sex, Drugs, and Rock 'n' Roll," *Rolling Stone*, May 5, 1988, p. 57.

26. Studs Terkel, *The Great Divide: Second Thoughts on the American Dream* (New York: Avon Books, 1988), p. 334.

27. Perry, p. 288.

28. Gottlieb, p. 187.

29. Gitlin, p. 429.

30. Gottlieb, pp. 304 and 312.

31. Terkel, pp. 137-38.

32. Katy Butler, "The Great Boomer Depression" *Mother Jones*, June 1989, 35.

33. Terkel, p. 124.

34. Walter Shapiro, "The Birth and—Maybe—Death of Yuppie-dom," *Time*, April 8, 1991, p. 65.

35. Kirk McNeill and Robert Paul, *Reaching for the Baby Boomers Workbook* (Nashville: The General Board of Discipleship of The United Methodist Church, 1989), pp. 11-14.

36. Drucker, pp. 188-90.

37. Weiss, pp. 268-392.

38. Ibid., p. 27.

39. Ibid., p. 30.

40. Ibid., p. 23.

41. Bob Sipchen, "Is America Losing Its Heart?," *Los Angeles Times*, January 17, 1991, p. E1.

42. Weiss, pp. 222-23.

43. William Grieder, "The Rolling Stone Survey: Portrait of a Generation," *Rolling Stone*, April 7, 1988, p. 36.

Chapter 4

1. Todd Gitlin, *The Sixties: Years of Hope, Days of Rage* (New York: Bantam Books, 1987), pp. 424-25.

2. Susan Littwin, *The Postponed Generation* (New York: William Morrow and Company, Inc., 1986), p. 24.

3. Ibid., p. 23.

4. Ibid.

5. *Information Please Almanac, 1990* (Boston: Houghton Mifflin Company Boston, 1990), p. 807.

6. Ibid., pp. 809-10.

7. Kathryn A. London and Barbara Foley Wilson, "Divorce," *American Demographics*, October 1988, p. 25.

8. Midge Decter, *Liberal Parents, Radical Children* (New York: Coward, McCann & Geoghegan, Inc., 1975), p. 34.

9. Kenneth L. Woodward, "Young Beyond Their Years," *Newsweek Special Edition, The 21st Century Family*, Winter/Spring 1990, p. 55.

10. Ibid.

11. Christopher Lasch, *The Culture of Narcissism* (New York: Warner Books, 1979), p. 38.

12. Ernest Becker, *The Denial of Death* (New York: The Free Press, 1973), p. 2.

13. Ibid., p. 3.

14. Ibid.

15. Michael Meyer, *The Alexander Complex* (New York: Times Books, 1989), pp. 36-37.

16. Becker, p. 5.

17. Madonna Kolbenschlag, *Lost in the Land of Oz* (San Francisco: Harper & Row, 1988), p. 127.

18. Ibid., p. 23.

19. Lester D. Langley, *MexAmerica* (New York: Crown Publishers, Inc., 1988), p. 284.

Chapter 5

1. Constant H. Jacquet, Jr., *Yearbook of American & Canadian Churches, 1989* (Nashville: Abingdon Press, 1989), pp. 252-53.

2. George Gallup, Jr. and Jim Castelli, *The People's Religion* (New York: Macmillan Publishing Company, 1989), p. 28.

3. Martha Farnsworth Riche, "Back to the Fifties," *American Demographics*, September 1988, p. 2. Reprinted with permission © American Demographics (Sept. 1988).

4. *Information Please Almanac, 1990* (Boston: Houghton Mifflin Company, 1990), p. 843.

5. Claudia Wallis, "Onward, Women," *Time*, December 4, 1989, p. 82.

6. Betty Friedan, *The Feminine Mystique, The Tenth Anniversary Edition* (New York: W. W. Norton & Company, 1974), p. 155.

7. U.S. Bureau of the Census, *Current Population Reports* Series P-25, No. 802, "Estimates of the Population of the United States."

8. J. Ronald Oakley, *God's Country: America in the Fifties* (New York: Dembner Books, 1986), p. 120.

9. Ibid., p. 117.

10. "Percent of Population Ever Married," Department of Commerce, Bureau of the Census, 1990.

11. Nancy Gibbs, "The Dreams of Youth," *Time Special Issue*, Fall, 1990, p. 14.

12. Friedan, p. 183.

13. Oakley, p. 294.

14. Wallis, p. 82.

15. Ibid., p. 295.

16. Friedan, pp. 44 and 77.

17. Sydney E. Ahlstrom, *A Religious History of the American People*, Vol. 2 (New York: Image Books, 1975), p. 450.

18. Oakley, p. 323.

19. Norman Vincent Peale, *The Power of Positive Thinking* (New York: Prentice-Hall, 1952), p. xi.

20. Ahlstrom, p. 452.

21. Ibid., p. 18.

22. Leonard I. Sweet, "The Modernization of Protestant Religion in America," *Altered Landscapes, Christianity in America, 1935-1985* (Grand Rapids, Michigan: William B. Eerdmans Publishing Company, 1989), p. 24.

23. Ibid., p. 30.

24. Ahlstrom, p. 461.

25. Sweet, pp. 30-31.

26. Tom Wolfe, "The Me Decade and the Third Great Awakening," *The Purple Decades* (New York: Berkeley Books, 1982), p. 282.

27. "The Jesus Movement Is Upon Us," *Look*, February 9, 1971, p. 15.

28. Chuck Smith and Tal Brooke, *Harvest* (Old Tappan, New Jersey: Chosen Books, 1987), p. 48.

29. Smith, pp. 15-16.

30. "The Gold Rush to Golgotha," *Time*, October 25, 1971, p. 65.

Chapter 6

1. Theodore Roszak, *The Making of a Counter Culture* (New York: Doubleday & Company, 1968), p. 217.

2. Roszak, p. 229.

3. Robert L. Johnson, "Protestant Hangups with the Counter-Culture," *The Christian Century*, November 4, 1970, pp. 1318-19.

4. Frank Trippett, "The Hesse Trip," *Look*, February 23, 1971, p. 56.

5. Tom Wolfe, "The Me Decade and the Third Great Awakening," *The Purple Decades* (New York: Berkeley Books, 1982), p. 280.

6. Ibid., p. 291.

7. George Gallup, Jr. and Jim Castelli, *The People's Religion* (New York: Macmillan Publishing Company, 1990), p. 13.

8. Jenny Jedeikin and Robert Love, "Maharishi's Magic Mountain," *Rolling Stone*, January 24, 1991, p. 9.

9. Russell Chandler, *Understanding the New Age* (Dallas: Word Publishing, 1988), pp. 60-61.

10. Ibid., p. 61.

11. Bob Sipchen and Jonathan Weisman, "Harmonic Convergence: A Braver New World?" *Los Angeles Times*, Wednesday, August 12, 1987, Part V, p. 4.

12. "A New Age Dawning," *Time*, August 31, 1987, p. 63.

13. "New Age Harmonies," *Time*, December 7, 1987, p. 62. Copyright © 1987 Time Warner Inc. Reprinted by permission.

14. John Naisbitt and Patricia Aburdene, *Megatrends 2000* (New York: William Morrow and Company, Inc., 1990), p. 293.

15. Lillie Wilson, "The Aging of Aquarius," *American Demograph-*

ics, September 1988, p. 34. Reprinted with permission. © American Demographics (September 1988).

16. Suzanne Doucet, "Success Has Diluted New Age Music," *Billboard*, June 18, 1988, p. 9. © 1988 BPI Communications, Inc. Used by permission from Billboard.

17. Blayne Cutler, "For What It's Worth," *American Demograpics*, August 1989, p. 44. Reprinted with permission. © American Demographics (Aug. 1989).

18. Gallup and Castelli, p. 131.

19. Chandler, p. 20.

20. Andrew Greeley, "Mysticism Goes Mainstream," *American Health*, January/February, 1987, pp. 47-49.

21. Ibid., p. 49.

22. Lillie Wilson, "The Aging of Aquarius," *American Demographics*, September 1988, p. 60.

23. Chandler, p. 21.

24. Gallup and Castelli, p. 126, report that 32 percent of charismatic baby boomers are age 18-29, and 29 percent are 30-49.

25. Craig Miller, "Interview with C. Peter Wagner," April 8, 1991.

26. Brad Edmondson, "Bringing in the Sheaves," *American Demographics*, August 1988, p. 31. Reprinted with permission. © American Demographics (Aug. 1988).

Chapter 7

1. Michael Maccoby, *Why Work: Motivating and Leading the New Generation* (New York: Touchstone Book, Simon & Schuster Inc., 1988), p. 46.

2. Ibid., p. 20.

3. Peter Drucker, *The New Realities* (New York, Harper & Row, Publishers, 1989), p. 94.

4. Ibid., p. 184.

5. John Naisbitt and Patricia Aburdene, *Megatrends 2000* (New York: William Morrow and Company, Inc., 1990), p. 298.

6. Dick Roraback, "650 Disciples Spend a Weekend in the Lives of Shirley MacLaine," *Los Angeles Times*, July 19, 1987, VI1.

7. J. Z. Knight, "First Word," *Omni*, March 1988, p. 8. Reprinted by permission of Omni, © 1988, Omni Publications International, Ltd.

8. James Patterson and Peter Kim, *The Day America Told the Truth* (New York: Prentice Hall Press, 1991), pp. 27-28.

9. Christopher Lasch, "Soul of a New Age," *Omni*, October, 1987, p. 82. Reprinted by permission of Omni, © 1987, Omni Publications International, Ltd.

10. Russell Chandler, *Understanding the New Age* (Dallas: Word Publishing, 1988), p. 62.

11. Lillie Wilson, "The Aging of Aquarius," *American Demographics*, September 1988, p. 36.

12. Ibid.

13. Allene Symons, "Inner Visions," *Publisher's Weekly*, September 25, 1987, p. 76.

14. Otto Friedrich, "New Age Harmonies," *Time*, December 7, 1987.

15. Marilyn Ferguson, *The Aquarian Conspiracy* (Los Angeles: J. P. Tarcher, Inc., 1980), p. 23.

16. Ibid., pp. 419-20.

17. Ibid., p. 419.

18. Frank Trippett, "The Hesse Trip," *Look*, February 23, 1971, pp. 54-55. Used by permission of Frank Trippett.

19. Gallup and Castelli, p. 46.

20. Ibid., pp. 88-89.

21. "The Empty Church Syndrome," *Psychology Today*, November 1989, p. 6.

22. Gallup and Castelli, pp. 60-61.

23. Russell Chandler, "Customer Poll Shapes a Church" *Los Angeles Times*, Monday, December 11, 1989, pp. A1 and A28-A31.

24. Bruce L. Bugbee, *Networking*, Fuller Institute, Pasadena, California.

25. Chris Meyer, "Missionary in Suburbia," *Valley News, South Orange County*, 1989, p. A20.

26. Russell Chandler, "Vineyard Fellowship Finds Groundswell of Followers," *Los Angeles Times*, October 5, 1990, p. A34.

27. John Wimber, "Zip to 3,000 in Five Years," Peter Wagner, *Signs & Wonders Today* (Altamonte Springs, Florida: Creation House, 1987), p. 31-34.

28. Craig Miller, "Interview with Steve Petty," March 20, 1990.

Chapter 8

1. Chellis Glendinning, *Waking Up in the Nuclear Age* (New York: Beech Tree Books, William Morrow, 1987), p. 81.

2. Annie Gottlieb, *Do You Believe in Magic? The Second Coming of the Sixties Generation* (New York: Times Books, 1987), p. 386.

3. Hal Lindsey, *The Late Great Planet Earth*, (Zondervan Publishing House, 1970), p. 43.

4. Ibid., p. 83.

5. Ibid., p. 60.

6. Ibid., p. 102.

7. Ibid., pp. 126-27.

8. Ibid., p. 167.

9. Ruth Montgomery and Joanne Garland, *Herald of the New Age* (New York: Fawcett Crest, 1986), pp. 233-34.

10. Jose Arguelles, *The Mayan Factor, Path Beyond Technology* (Santa Fe, New Mexico: Bear & Company, 1987), p. 189.

11. Ibid.

12. Ibid., p. 190.

13. Ibid.

14. Ibid., p. 193.

15. Ibid., pp. 194 and 196.

16. Ann Japenga, "A Test of Faith," *Los Angeles Times*, March 29, 1990, E1.

17. Hillel Schwartz, *Century's End* (New York: Doubleday, 1990), p. 9.

18. Richard Erdoes, "The Year 1000," *Psychology Today*, May 1989, pp. 44-45.

19. Bob Drogin, "Hotshots in Kuwait's Fiery Hell," *Los Angeles Times*, April 3, 1991, p. A8.

20. Micheal Parks, "Chernobyl," *Los Angeles Times*, April 23, 1991, pp. H1 & H6.

21. Janice Castro, "Who Knows How Many Will Die?," *Time*, April 29, 1991, p. 64.

22. Maura Dolan and Larry B. Stammer, "Planet Worse Off Since First Earth Day in 1970," *Los Angeles Times*, April 15, 1990, p. 1.

23. "4.6 billion pounds of toxic chemicals released in 1988," *The Orange County Register*, April 20, 1990, p. A12.

24. Kathleen Hendrix, "Vanishing Forest Fells Way of Life," *Los Angeles Times*, March 18, 1990, p. 1.

25. Dolan and Stammer, p. 1.

26. Anastasia Toufexis, "Too Many Mouths," *Time*, January 2, 1989, p. 48.

27. "Environmental Refugees," *USA Today*, April 1989, p. 6.

28. Russell Chandler, "Religious Join the Crusade to Save Earth from Pollution," *Los Angeles Times*, April 19, 1990, p. A3.

29. Ibid.

30. David G. Savage, "1 in 4 Young Blacks in Jail or in Court Control, Study Says," *Los Angeles Times*, February 27, 1990, p. A16.

31. Gordon Witkin, "Kids Who Kill," *U.S. News & World Report*, April 8, 1991, pp. 28-29.

32. Paul Leiberman, "When L.A. Gangs Move In," *Los Angeles Times*, February 4, 1990, p. A3.

33. Mortimer B. Zuckerman, "Why America Slept," *U.S. News & World Report*, February 26, 1990, p. 67. Used by permission.

34. Elizabeth Mehren, "With the End of War Comes Ho-Hum Reality," *Los Angeles Times*, March 11, 1991, p. E1.

Chapter 9

1. Joe Schwartz and Thomas Exter, "American Demographics," May 1989, p. 36. Reprinted with permission. © American Demographics (May 1989).

2. Lori Grange, "Armenian Becomes Top Foreign Tongue in Glendale Schools," *Los Angeles Times*, May 13, 1990, p. J6.

3. "A New Snapshot for Our Schools," *Los Angeles Times Orange County Edition*, April 11, 1991, p. B10.

4. David Gergen, "The Future of the Melting Pot," *U.S. News & World Report*, April 8, 1991, p. 35.

5. Schwartz and Exter, p. 36.

6. Peter F. Drucker, *The New Realities* (New York: Harper & Row, Publishers, 1989), p. 256.

7. Ibid., pp. 256-57.

8. Craig Miller, "Interview with Peter Wagner," April 8, 1991.

9. Joseph Campbell, *The Power of Myth*, (New York: Doubleday, 1988), pp. 141-42.

10. Ibid., p. 9.

11. Thomas H. Troeger, *Imagining a Sermon* (Nashville: Abingdon Press, 1990), p. 26.

12. Ibid., p. 122.

13. Ibid., p. 120.

14. Connie Koenenn, "Technostress," *Los Angeles Times*, May 11, 1990, p. E1.

15. Ibid., p. E6.

16. Drucker, p. 116.

17. Ibid., p. 123.

18. John Naisbitt and Patricia Aburdene, *Megatrends 2000* (New York: William Morrow and Company, Inc., 1990), p. 178.

19. Ibid., p. 179.

20. Ibid., p. 208.

21. Percentages based on figures from: David B. Barrett, "Annual Statistical Table on Global Mission: 1991," *International Bulletin of Missionary Research*, January 1991, p. 25.

22. Ibid.
23. Ibid., p. 61.
24. Ibid., pp. 64-65.
25. Paul Yonggi Cho, *The Fourth Dimension* (South Plainsfield, NJ: Publishing, Inc.,), p. 44.
26. Barrett, p. 25.
27. William Greider, "The Rolling Stone Survey," *Rolling Stone,* April 7, 1988, p. 35.
28. Ibid, p. 36.
29. James Fallows, *More Like Us, Making America Great Again* (Boston: Houghton Mifflin Company, 1989), p. 2.
30. Ibid., pp. 11-12.
31. Ibid., p. 12.
32. Coretta Scott King, *The Words of Martin Luther King, Jr.* (New York: Newmarket Press, 1987), p. 97.

Chapter 10

1. Jeff Ostroff, "Targeting the Prime-Life Consumer," *American Demographics,* January 1991, p. 30.
2. "Fertility Indicators, 1920-1989," U.S. Department of Commerce, Bureau of the Census, 1990.
3. Jill Smolowe, "Last Call For Motherhood," *Time,* Fall 1990, p. 25.
4. "Fertility of American Women: June 1988," U.S. Department of Commerce, Bureau of the Census, p. 4.
5. Ibid., p. 76.
6. Rebecca Piirto, "New Women's Revolution," *American Demographics,* April 1991, p. 6.
7. Jennifer McEnroe, "Split-Shift Parenting," *American Demographics,* February 1991, p. 52.
8. Sam Allis, "What Do Men Really Want?," *Time,* Fall 1990, p. 81.
9. Ibid.
10. David E. Bloom, "Women and Work," *American Demographics,* September, 1986, pp. 25-26.
11. Pat Wingert and Barbar Kantrowitz, "The Day Care Generation," *Newsweek Special Issue,* Winter/Spring 1990, p. 87. © 1990 Newsweek, Inc. All rights reserved. Reprinted by permission.
12. Ibid., p. 89.
13. McEnroe, pp. 50, 52.
14. "Proportion of Two-Parent Family Households Has Decreased Dramatically Since 1970, Census Bureau Reports," *United States Commerce News,* January 30, 1991.

15. Claudia Wallis, "Onward, Women!", *Time,* December 4, 1989, p. 85.

16. Johnathan Kozil, "The New Untouchables," *Newsweek Special Issue, The 21st Century Family,* Winter/Spring 1990, p. 49.

17. Itabari Njeri, "Beyond the Melting Pot," *Los Angeles Times,* January 13, 1991, p. E1.

18. Janice Castro, "Get Set: Here They Come!," *Time,* Fall 1990, p. 52.

19. Ibid.

20. Joe Schwartz, "The Baby Boom Talks to the Dead," *American Demographics,* April 1991, p. 14.

21. James Patterson and Peter Kim, *The Day America Told the Truth* (New York: Prentice-Hall Press, 1991), pp. 204-05.

22. Frank E. Peretti, *The Present Darkness* (Westchester, Illinois: Crossway Books, 1989), pp. 44-45.

23. Craig Miller, "Interview with Scott Young," April 29, 1991.

24. Ken Dychtwald and Joe Flower, *Age Wave* (Los Angeles: Jeremy P. Tarcher, Inc., 1986), p. 21.

25. Cheryl Russell, *100 Predictions for the Baby Boom* (New York: Plenum Press, 1987), pp. 206-07.

26. Kirk McNeill and Robert Paul, *Reaching for the Baby Boomers Workbook* (Nashville, TN: The General Board of Discipleship of The United Methodist Church, 1989), p. 17

27. Dychtwald and Flower pp. 6-9.

28. Ibid., p. 68.

29. Matthew Greenwald, "Bad News for the Baby Boomers," *American Demographics,* February 1989, p. 34.

30. Ibid., p. 36.

31. Dychtwald and Flower, p. 9.

32. James Ogilvy, "Experience Industry," *American Demographics,* December 1986, pp. 27-28.

33. Steven Phillips, "King Customer," *Business Week,* March 12, 1990, p. 88.

34. Anna Quindlen, "And Now, A Word from One of Them," *Business Month,* October, 1987, p. 27.

35. George Gallup, Jr., *The People's Religion* (New York: Macmillan Publishing Company, 1989), p. 130.

36. Patterson and Kim, pp. 199-200.

37. Craig Miller, "Interview with C. Peter Wagner," April 8, 1991.

38. Craig Miller, "Interview with Bill Bray," April 26, 1991.

39. Ted Holden and James B. Treece, "Amway's Big, Happy Family Is All Smiles—In Japan," *Business Week,* September 4, 1989, p. 47.

40. Carl F. George, "Meta-Church, the Church of the Future," *The*

Pastor's Update, Charles E. Fuller Institute of Evangelism & Church Growth, January 1991, p. 3.

41. Craig Miller, "Interview with Mickey Elliott," April 29, 1991.

42. Janice Castro, "The Simple Life," *Time,* April 8, 1991, p. 58.

43. Peter F. Drucker, *The New Realities* (New York: Harper & Row, Publishers, 1989), p. 198.

44. Patterson and Kim, p. 230.

45. Drucker, p. 198.

46. Ibid., p. 205.

INDEX